Hyatt Legal Services

Home Lawyer™

Reference Manual

MECA Software, Inc.
55 Walls Drive
Fairfield, CT 06430-0912

OverDrive Systems, Inc.
23980 Chagrin Blvd.
Suite 200
Cleveland, OH 44122

TRADEMARKS

Home Lawyer is a registered trademark of OverDrive Systems, Inc.
IBM, PC, XT and AT are registered trademarks of International Business Machines Corporation.
MECA is a trademark of MECA Software, Inc.

ACKNOWLEDGMENTS

Program Design & Development: Robert Bourne, Ken Clark, Rachel McKenzie, M. Steven Potash, Tom Skiba

Product Marketing: Monica Jackson, Kent L. Johnson, Laureen DiCaprio Kinkopf

Reference Manual Editor: Ann Russell

Legal Document Authors and Editors: Martha Denney, Joseph W. Mierzwa, MaryEllen Tymoszczuk, and the staff of Hyatt Legal Services

Product Support and Testing: Laureen DiCaprio Kinkopf, John Mamrak, Karen Sharp Snodgrass, Paul Zaepfel

Support, Guidance and Leadership: Geoffrey Boguch, Pat Carney, Sidney Dwarkin, Sidney Franklin, Michael Freidman, Barbara Gold, Stephen Gold, Michael Hartzmark, Joel Hyatt, Jill A. Milkovich, Joanne Parrino, Ken Podor, Bernie Potash, Loree Potash, Herb Rosen, Edward Rosenthal, Dan Schley, Ron Schreiber, Ed Siegel, Frank Slovenec, Wayne G. Willis

Second Edition
Hyatt Legal Services
Home Lawyer
Version 2.01
March 1992

Important Notice Regarding Home Lawyer Documents

The documents included in this product can be used to handle the simple legal matters encountered by the typical family in everyday life. This product provides examples and prompts -- in plain, simple English -- to enable you to create a will, power of attorney or other documents suitable for your needs.

Your use of this product does not create an attorney-client relationship between you and Hyatt Legal Services, MECA Software, Inc. or OverDrive Systems, Inc. You may need a lawyer for your particular matter. It is your right and option to consult with one.

Be aware that laws and procedures do vary from state to state and may change. They may also be interpreted differently by different people. Furthermore, there is no way to identify that you fully understand the reasons for the questions asked, that you have accurately followed the directions provided or that the result you intend can or will be met by the documents you find in this product. As a result, neither Hyatt Legal Services, OverDrive Systems, Inc. nor MECA Software, Inc., guarantees or warrants that the documents created with this Program will be valid at the time you use them, will lead to the result you desire or will carry out your intentions. Neither Hyatt Legal Services, OverDrive Systems, Inc. nor MECA Software, Inc. accepts any responsibility or liability for a document which is incorrectly used or inaccurately completed.

These documents are to be used only by you for personal legal matters. Our aim is to assist you to "do it yourself." Recognize, however, that if you do not understand the effect of the document you choose or if you are confused by any of the document's provisions, you should consult with an attorney in your state for assistance and advice. Discussing your concerns with an attorney may be essential to your full understanding of your rights and options. Toward that end, a list of state sponsored attorney referral programs is enclosed in this package for your reference. This list is provided for your convenience and is not intended to be an endorsement of the Product by these Bar Associations.

OverDrive Systems, Inc.
MECA Software, Inc.

Plain Language License

About This Product and Your Rights

This product (disks, manual, etc.) is protected by United States copyright laws. You are not allowed to make copies of the product for anyone else or for more than one computer. You may make a copy for your own safekeeping (backup).

OverDrive Systems, Inc. and MECA Software, Inc. guarantee that the disks will be free of defects but do not make any other warranties. If you find a disk is defective, we will replace it during the first 90 days. Send us the bad disk and your receipt for the Product and we'll send you a new disk or refund your money. This agreement is controlled by Ohio law.

THIS WARRANTY IS IN PLACE OF ALL OTHER WARRANTIES. OVERDRIVE SYSTEMS, INC. AND MECA SOFTWARE, INC. MAKE NO OTHER WARRANTIES OF ANY KIND, EITHER EXPRESS OR IMPLIED, INCLUDING WITHOUT LIMITATION ANY WARRANTY OF MERCHANTABILITY OR FITNESS FOR A PARTICULAR PURPOSE. OVERDRIVE SYSTEMS, INC. AND MECA SOFTWARE, INC. ARE NOT LIABLE FOR ANY INCIDENTAL OR CONSEQUENTIAL DAMAGES ARISING FROM YOUR USE OR INABILITY TO USE THE PROGRAM. OVERDRIVE SYSTEMS, INC.'S AND MECA SOFTWARE, INC.'S LIABILITY IN NO EVENT SHALL EXCEED THE AMOUNT YOU PAID FOR THE PROGRAM.

If you have any questions regarding this Agreement, you may contact MECA Software, Inc. by writing or calling at the following address:

MECA Software, Inc.
55 Walls Drive
Fairfield, CT 06430-0912

1-800-288-MECA

Dear Home Lawyer User,

Thank you for purchasing Home Lawyer. You have taken an important step in protecting the rights of yourself and your family.

Home Lawyer is designed to be very easy to use. You can prepare your will or other important documents quickly and easily from the comfort of your own home.

Knowing your legal rights is important -- and Home Lawyer is the right choice in helping you to protect them. All of us at Hyatt Legal Services hope this product will bring you and your family an added measure of security and peace of mind.

You have my word on it!

Sincerely,

Joel Hyatt[*]

---

[*] Hyatt Legal Services is named after its founder, Joel Z. Hyatt, who is admitted to practice law personally in Ohio only.

Contents

Chapter 1 Introduction

1-1   Introduction
1-1   What is Home Lawyer?
1-1   Hyatt Legal Services
1-2   Home Lawyer Documents
1-2   Document Table of Contents
1-5   About the Home Lawyer Advisor
1-5   The Advisor Menu

Chapter 2 Getting Started

2-1   Getting Started
2-1   Contents of This Package
2-1   Installing Home Lawyer
2-2   Structure of This Manual

Chapter 3 Using Home Lawyer

3-1   Using Help
3-3   Moving Around with a Mouse
3-4   Moving Around with the Keyboard
3-5   Steps to Using Home Lawyer
3-6   Documents Menu
    3-6   Document Table of Contents
    3-7   Selecting a Document
    3-8   Document Descriptions
    3-8   Question and Answer Session
    3-8   Entering an Answer
    3-10   Editing Key Summary
    3-11   Entering States
    3-11   Entering Dates
    3-11   Selecting a Response
    3-12   Changing an Answer
    3-12   Saving Your Answers
    3-14   Using Your Saved Answers
3-16   File Menu
    3-16   Print Document
        3-18   Printing to a Printer
        3-18   Print Document to Screen
        3-19   Printing to a File

3-22   Product Information
     3-23   Register Your Program
     3-23   MECA Software
     3-23   Customer Support
3-24   Setup
     3-24   User Profile
     3-26   System Setup
     3-27   About
3-27   DOS Shell
3-27   Exit
3-28 Edit Menu
     3-29   Edit Answers
     3-29   Review Answers
     3-30   Print Worksheets
     3-33   Shell to WP
3-34 Advisor Menu
     3-35   Preventive Law Interview
     3-35   Personal Law Topics
          3-36   Expand
          3-37   Explain
          3-38   Print
          3-39   Cancel
     3-39   Glossary of Terms
     3-40   State Bar Associations

Chapter 4   Home Lawyer Advisor

4-1   Personal Law Interview
     4-1   Document Summary
     4-1   Questions and Comments
4-5   Personal Law Topics
     4-5   Chapter 1 -- Wills and Trusts
     4-6   Chapter 2 -- Owning Your Own Home
     4-6   Chapter 3 -- Landlords and Tenants
     4-7   Chapter 4 -- You, Your Family, and the Law
     4-7   Chapter 5 -- Divorce and Custody
     4-8   Chapter 6 -- Consumers' Rights
     4-8   Chapter 7 -- Your Job or Business
     4-9   Chapter 8 -- Your Credit
     4-9   Chapter 9 -- You and Your Automobile
     4-10   Chapter 10 -- Medical Rights
     4-10   Chapter 11 -- Going to Court
     4-11   Chapter 12 -- When You Need A Lawyer

Chapter 5   Wills and Living Wills

    5-1   Estate Planning Worksheet

          5-1   Document Summary

          5-2   Questions and Comments

          5-7   Sample Document

    5-8   Last Will and Testament

          5-8   Document Summary

          5-9   Special Considerations

          5-11   Questions and Comments

          5-27   Sample Document

    5-34   Living Will

          5-34   Document Summary

          5-36   Questions and Comments

          5-40   Sample Document

    5-42   Revocation of Living Will

          5-42   Document Summary

          5-42   Questions and Comments

          5-45   Sample Document

Chapter 6   Powers of Attorney

    6-1   General Power of Attorney

          6-1   Document Summary

          6-3   Questions and Comments

          6-8   Sample Document

    6-12   Medical/Special Power of Attorney

          6-12   Document Summary

          6-14   Questions and Comments

          6-19   Sample Document

    6-22   Revocation of Power of Attorney

          6-22   Document Summary

          6-23   Questions and Comments

          6-25   Sample Document

Chapter 7   Employment Forms

    7-1   Employment Agreement

          7-1   Document Summary

          7-2   Questions and Comments

          7-6   Sample Document

    7-9   Independent Contractor Agreement

          7-9   Document Summary

          7-10   Questions and Comments

          7-15   Sample Document

7-17   Offer of Employment Letter
      7-17   Document Summary
      7-17   Questions and Comments
      7-22   Sample Document

Chapter 8   Credit and Collections

8-1   Credit and Collections
      8-1   Promissory Note
      8-1   Document Summary
      8-3   Questions and Comments
      8-10 Sample Document
8-13 Demand for Money Owed
      8-13 Document Summary
      8-13 Questions and Comments
      8-18 Sample Document
8-19 Bad Check Notice
      8-19 Document Summary
      8-19 Questions and Comments
      8-23 Sample Document
8-24 Request for Credit Report
      8-24 Document Summary
      8-24 Questions and Comments
      8-30 Sample Document
8-31 Request for Credit Report Correction
      8-31 Document Summary
      8-31 Questions and Comments
      8-34 Sample Document

Chapter 9   Bills of Sale

9-1   Motor Vehicle Bill of Sale
      9-1   Document Summary
      9-2   Questions and Comments
      9-6   Sample Document
9-8   General Bill of Sale
      9-8   Document Summary
      9-9   Questions and Comments
      9-12 Sample Document

Chapter 10   Residential Lease

10-1 Residential Lease
      10-1 Document Summary
      10-2 Questions and Comments
      10-10 Sample Document

Chapter 11   **Defective Product Complaint Letter**
11-1   Defective Product Complaint Letter
        11-1   Document Summary
        11-1   Questions and Comments
        11-6   Sample Document

Appendices   A-1   Terminology
                  B-1   Error Messages
                  C-1   Customer Support Plan
                  D-1   State Bar Associations

Index

What is Home Lawyer?

Home Lawyer is a personal legal software product that lets you create, change or update frequently-needed documents like a simple will, power of attorney and sales agreement from the comfort of your own home. Home Lawyer contains important documents from Hyatt Legal Services, the nation's largest general practice law firm. Hyatt Legal Services selected the documents used most often in protecting the rights of their clients.

Not too long ago, you had to go all the way downtown, perhaps missing a day of work, to see your attorney. You may have spent hours discussing a simple document, only to discover that you needed to schedule another appointment. Worse yet, your attorney's meter started running the minute you walked through the door.

Those days are over!

Home Lawyer makes creating documents as easy as turning on your home computer. Home Lawyer guides you step-by-step through each document by asking a series of questions. And Home Lawyer talks to you in plain English -- not confusing legalese. Answer the questions and Home Lawyer automatically creates a document suited to your individual needs.

Hyatt Legal Services

Joel Hyatt, founder and Senior Partner of Hyatt Legal Services, opened the first office in 1977 with a goal to make legal services affordable and accessible to middle-income Americans. He wanted to make the legal system work for a vast segment of the population whose needs were previously unmet. So he located his law offices in convenient neighborhood shopping centers. He kept them open in the evenings and on Saturdays so clients wouldn't have to miss work to see their attorney. Hyatt's clients received written estimates for the cost of Hyatt's services up front. And he advertised on television so that many people could learn about this new kind of law firm which understood their needs.

Today, Hyatt Legal Services is making the legal system work for more people in more states than any other law firm in the country. Hyatt has more than 100 offices in 15 states and the District of Columbia.

Unfortunately, studies still indicate that an alarming number of Americans avoid seeking legal advice because they fear the cost and do not know where to find a suitable attorney. Home Lawyer addresses those problems by bringing the collective wisdom of Hyatt Legal Services' attorneys into your home for a one-time price you can afford. Now, valuable and important documents like wills, powers of attorney and promissory notes are at your fingertips -- convenient, affordable and accessible.

Home Lawyer Documents

Document Table of Contents

♦ Wills and Living Wills

■ Estate Planning Worksheet

A personal interview which guides you through a series of questions to determine the value of your estate for estate planning purposes.

■ Last Will & Testament

Your Last Will and Testament contains your instructions regarding the disposition of your property after your death. If you die without leaving a will, the laws of your state will determine what happens to your property.

■ Living Will

This document is a directive to physicians, instructing them of your desire to have life-prolonging measures withheld or withdrawn in the event of a terminal illness.

■ Revocation of Living Will

This document is used to revoke a previously executed living will.

♦ Powers of Attorney

■ General Power of Attorney

This document allows one individual (the principal) to give another (the attorney-in-fact) broad and wide-ranging powers regarding the personal affairs and property of the principal.

■ Medical/Special Power of Attorney

This document allows one individual (the principal) to give another (the attorney-in-fact) specific powers regarding the personal affairs and property of the principal. It may be used to authorize medical care and treatment for the minor children of the principal; to authorize the sale or transfer of real estate on the principal's behalf; or to provide for the sale of items of the principal's personal property.

■ Revocation of Power of Attorney

This document is used to revoke a previously executed power of attorney.

♦ Employment Forms

■ Employment Agreement

Agreement for one individual to be employed by a business or organization.

■ Independent Contractor Agreement

Agreement for one individual to serve as an independent contractor or consultant for a business organization.

■ Offer of Employment Letter

Letter specifying terms of employment.

♦ Credit and Collections

■ Promissory Note

This document obligates one party (the Maker) to pay money to another (the Payee).

■ Demand Letter for Money Owed

Final demand for money owed.

■ Bad Check Notice

Letter notifying a person owing you money that he or she wrote an NSF (no or insufficient funds) check.

■ Request for Credit Report

Letter requesting a credit report (also called a credit record or profile) from a local credit bureau.

■ Request for Credit Report Correction

Letter requesting a local credit bureau to correct your credit report.

♦ Bills of Sale

■ Bill of Sale for Motor Vehicle

Document for transferring the title of an automobile or other motor vehicle.

■ General Bill of Sale

Document for transferring ownership of personal property.

♦ Residential Lease

Agreement for the leasing of residential property. This document is appropriate for most residential leasing situations.

♦ Defective Product Complaint Letter

Consumer complaint to a store or manufacturer regarding a defective product.

For a complete description of each document see the Document Summary in Chapters 5 through 11.

About the Home Lawyer Advisor

The Advisor Menu

In order to help you make the most of Home Lawyer, we'd like to suggest that you take a few minutes to acquaint yourself with the Home Lawyer Advisor.

Home Lawyer's *Preventive Law Interview* is designed to help you identify the documents you are most likely to need. When you answer the Preventive Law Interview questions, you'll be directed to the appropriate documents in the program.

You'll also be given directions to topics of interest in Home Lawyer's *Personal Law Topics*. The Advisor contains information about the law and its impact on many areas of your life, from home ownership to estate planning, from family law to buying and selling an automobile.

For further information about the Home Lawyer Advisor, see Chapter 4.

Getting Started

Before you begin, check to make sure you have everything you need. Home Lawyer will operate on any IBM PC, XT, AT or PS/2 compatible computer with at least 512K of RAM (memory) and a hard disk. The documents can be printed using any IBM compatible printer.

Contents of This Package

This package contains two 5 1/4" diskettes and one 3 1/2" diskette. The disks contain the installation program and system files.

Also included are the following items:
- Product Registration Card
- Easy-to-use Reference Manual
- Quick Reference Card
- Important Document Envelope
- Disk Envelope

Installing Home Lawyer

■ Make sure the DOS prompt is on your screen (e.g. C:\). Place Home Lawyer *Disk 1* into Drive A.

■ Change to your drive containing Home Lawyer *Disk 1*. For example, type **A:** and press [Enter].

■ Type **INSTALL** and press [Enter]. Follow the instructions on the screen.

The installation procedure automatically creates an \HL2 directory (unless you specify otherwise) and copies program files to your hard disk.

■ From the root directory (e.g. C:\), type **HL** and press [Enter].

Hint: You can also start Home Lawyer from the \HL2 directory. Type **CD \HL2** and press [Enter].

The Home Lawyer Main Menu appears on the screen. You are now ready to begin!

Structure of This Manual

Chapter 1 contains an overview of Home Lawyer and Hyatt Legal Services. Chapter 2 has information about the contents of this package and how to install and use Home Lawyer. Chapter 3 describes the features of Home Lawyer and gives instructions on completing a document and using the Home Lawyer Advisor.

Chapter 4 describes the benefits of the Advisor and how to use it. Chapters 5 through 11 contain detailed information about each document and additional instructions for completing it.

The Appendices include a glossary of terms, a list of error messages, a directory of State Bar Associations and state abbreviations. They also include information about our Customer Support Plan.

To find information, refer to either the main Table of Contents or the detailed Index at the end of this manual.

Moving Around with the Keyboard

There are four different types of selectors: Menus, Menu options, List Boxes, and Buttons. Each is selected differently.

■ There are two ways to select a Menu from the Menu Bar (e.g., File Menu):

1. First, press [Alt] and the first letter of the command name (i.e. [Alt-F] for the File Menu). This will pull down the Menu and display the Menu options.

2. Second, press the [Alt] key and use the left and right arrow keys to highlight the menu command (i.e. File, Edit, Documents, Advisor) and [Enter] to display the Menu options.

■ To select a Menu option (e.g., Print Document from the File Menu), use the arrow keys to highlight the desired option and [Enter] to execute.

Hint: Type the first letter of the option to quickly jump to that option.

■ To select from a List Box (e.g., the Help Topics), use the arrow keys to highlight the desired choice and [Enter] to select.

Hint: Type the first letter of your selection to quickly jump to that selection.

■ To select a Button, (i.e. <OK> or <CANCEL>), use the [Tab], [Shift-Tab] or arrow keys to highlight the desired Button and [Enter] to execute.

■ To position the cursor in an Entry or Edit field, use the [Tab], [Shift-Tab] or arrow keys to highlight the desired Button and the space bar to select.

■■■■■■■■

**Moving Around
with a Mouse**

There are four different types of selectors: Menus, Menu options, List Boxes, and Buttons. Each is selected differently.

■ To select a Menu from the menu bar (e.g., File Menu) move the mouse until the pointer is positioned on the desired menu and click the left button on the mouse.

This will pull down the menu and display the menu options.

■ To select a Menu option (e.g., Print Document from the File Menu) move the mouse until the pointer is positioned on the desired option and click the left button on the mouse to execute.

■ There are two ways to select from a List Box (e.g., Help Index):

1. First, move the mouse pointer until the pointer is positioned on the desired selection and double click the left button on the mouse. This will immediately highlight and execute the selection.

2. Second, move the mouse pointer until the pointer is positioned on the desired selection and click the left button on the mouse. Then move the mouse until the pointer is positioned on the desired action and click the left button on the mouse. Click once for a Button and twice for a Menu option (i.e. single click on an <OK> or <CANCEL> Button or double click on a Menu option such as *Edit Answers* from the Edit Menu).

■ To select a Button (i.e. <OK> or <CANCEL>) move the mouse pointer to the desired Button and click the left button on the mouse. This will select and execute the Button.

■ To position the cursor in an Entry or Edit field, move the mouse until the pointer is on the desired field and click the left mouse button. The cursor will position itself in the entry field and you may begin typing.

- [PgUp] and [PgDn] to review the help information.

- [Home] to quickly move to the first Help Topic.

- [End] to quickly move to the last Help Topic.

- [Esc] to return to the Help Menu.

- [Esc] again to quit Help.

Using Help

With Home Lawyer's on-line help you have immediate access to information about the use of the program as well as additional comments about the documents and questions.

■ Press [Alt-H] to display the Help Menu.

■ Highlight the desired topic and [Enter] to select.

Select *Help Topics* for information about the use of Home Lawyer.

Select *Welcome New User* for important information to first-time users of the product.

If you select Help Topics, a list of topics appears.

Help Topics Index

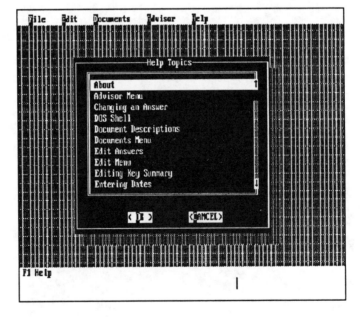

■ Using the arrow keys, highlight the desired topic and [Enter] to select.

Steps to Using Home Lawyer

Step 1 Review Welcome New User

Step 2 Complete User Profile

Step 3 Complete the Personal Law Interview

Step 4 Review related topics in the Personal Law Topics

Step 5 Select the document from the Documents Menu

Step 6 Enter information through the Question and Answer Screen and review your answers making changes as needed

Step 7 Print the completed document to the screen or printer

Documents Menu

Home Lawyer provides eighteen frequently needed documents and letters prepared by Hyatt Legal Services for your use at home.

Document Table of Contents

- ♦ **Wills and Living Wills**
    - ■ Estate Planning Worksheet
    - ■ Last Will and Testament
    - ■ Living Will
    - ■ Revocation of Living Will

- ♦ **Powers of Attorney**
    - ■ General Power of Attorney
    - ■ Medical/Special Power of Attorney
    - ■ Revocation of Power of Attorney

- ♦ **Employment Forms**
    - ■ Employment Agreement
    - ■ Independent Contractor Agreement
    - ■ Offer of Employment Letter

- ♦ **Credit and Collections**
    - ■ Promissory Note
    - ■ Demand for Money Owed
    - ■ Bad Check Notice
    - ■ Request for Credit Report
    - ■ Request for Credit Report Correction

- ♦ **Bills of Sale**
    - ■ Motor Vehicle Bill of Sale
    - ■ General Bill of Sale

- ♦ **Residential Lease**

- ♦ **Defective Product Complaint Letter**

The Documents Menu contains the following:

Documents Menu

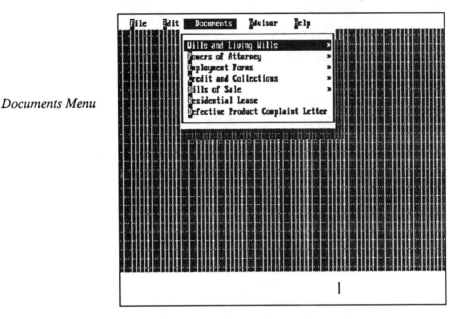

■ To select the Documents Menu, press [Alt-D] or point and click using a mouse.

Selecting a Document

■ If the Documents Menu is not displayed, press [Alt-D] or point and click on Documents using a mouse.

■ To select a document, highlight the document using the arrow keys and [Enter] or point and click using a mouse.

A document title followed by a chevron (») indicates a chapter of documents. Selecting a chapter will display a window listing additional documents ready to select.

If the highlight bar is located on the first document, you can move quickly to the last document by using the Up Arrow key.

If the highlight bar is located on the last document, you can move quickly to the first document by using the Down Arrow Key.

Document Descriptions

■ If the Document Menu is not displayed, press [Alt-D] or point and click using a mouse.

■ Highlight the desired document and press [F1] More About This Document for a description of the document.

■ Use the [PgUp] and [PgDn] keys to move through each screen of text or the up and down arrow keys to scroll.

■ [Esc] to clear.

Question and Answer Session

After a document is selected, the Question and Answer session leads you through a series of screens with questions which must be answered to properly complete a document.

The Question and Answer Screen is divided into three sections:

1. Question and Example

2. Comments

3. Response Area

Entering an Answer

■ If the Question requires an answer from the keyboard, simply begin typing.

■ If you make a mistake while typing an answer, you can correct your answer using the backspace, delete or insert keys. You can also use the [F2] key to erase your entry and start over (see Editing Key Summary).

■ If the Question requires a selection from a list of responses, use the arrow keys to highlight your choice or point and click using a mouse.

■ [Alt-N], [Enter] or [F10] moves you forward through the questions or point and click on <NEXT> using a mouse.

■ [Alt-P] or [F9] moves you to the previous question or point and click on <PREV> using a mouse.

■ If [F1] Additional Comments appears on the prompt line at the bottom of the screen, there are additional comments for that question. Press [F1] to display.

Editing Key Summary

[F1]	Help More About Document Additional Comments
[F2]	Clear Field
[F9]	Move to Previous Question
[F10]	Move to Next Question
<Prev>	Move to Previous Question
<Next>	Move to Next Question
<Cancel>	Return to Previous Menu or Quit
[Bksp]	Delete character to left of cursor
[Del]	Delete character cursor is on
[Enter]	Accept answer, move to next question or line
[Esc]	Return to Previous Menu or Quit
[Home]	Move to beginning of line in Response Area
[End]	Move to end of line in Response Area
[Ctrl-Home]	Move to first character in Response Area
[Ctrl-End]	Move to last character in Response Area
[Ins]	Toggles OverType on/off
[PgDn]	Page Down Print to Screen/Review/Help Window
[PgUp]	Page Up Print to Screen/Review/Help Window
[Arrows]	Move cursor left/right on character Move cursor up/down one line or menu option
[Alt-A]	Display Advisor Menu
[Alt-C]	Cancel
[Alt-D]	Display Documents Menu
[Alt-E]	Display Edit Menu
[Alt-F]	Display File Menu
[Alt-H]	Display Help Menu
[Alt-N]	Move to the next question
[Alt-P]	Move to the previous question

Entering States

When a question asks for the name of a state, use the two-letter abbreviation. Home Lawyer will automatically convert the two-letter abbreviation to the entire name when necessary (e.g., WA will convert to Washington).

- If you are unsure of the state abbreviation, press [F1] *Help* and highlight *State Abbreviations*. Press [Enter].

- [Esc] to quit Help.

Entering Dates

All dates are entered in the MM/DD/YY or MM/DD/YYYY format. Home Lawyer will automatically convert it to words when needed in the completed document (e.g. 09/28/90 will convert to September 28, 1990).

For some questions, Home Lawyer automatically suggests the system date (the current date entered in your computer).

- Press [Enter] or point and click on <Next> to use the suggested date and continue to the next question.

- To change the suggested date, type over the existing date or press [F2] to clear.

Selecting a Response

Some questions require selecting an answer from a list. You will be asked to select the desired option.

- Using the arrow keys or [Tab], highlight the desired response or point and click using a mouse.

- Press [Enter] or point and click on <Next> using a mouse.

The program accepts the answer and moves on to the next question.

Changing an Answer

If you have already moved on to the next Question and want to correct or change a previous answer, you have two choices:

1.   Press [F9] or point and click on <PREV> to move back question by question. Use the editing keys to make changes (see *Editing Key Summary*). When the change is complete, press [F10] or point and click on <NEXT> to move forward.

2.   At the end of a Question and Answer session, you can edit your answers. See *Edit Answers*.

Saving Your Answers

When you have completed the Question and Answer session, a prompt appears asking you to save your answers.

Save Answers Prompt

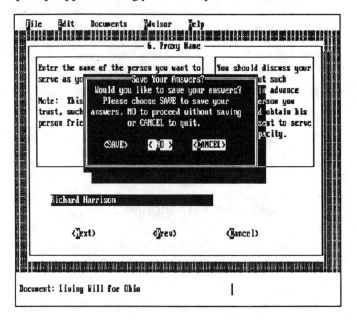

Select *SAVE* to save your answers.

Select *NO* to quit the Questions and Answer session without saving your answers.

Select *CANCEL* to return to the question and answer screen.

■ Press [Tab] or the arrow keys to highlight the desired choice and [Enter] or point and click using a mouse.

If you select SAVE, the following Menu appears.

Save Answers

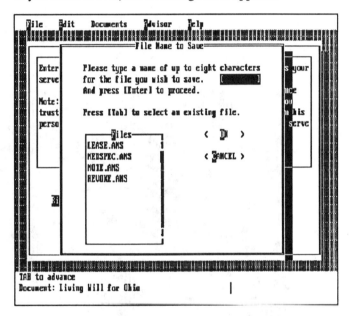

The current answer file will automatically appear in the entry field.

■ To save to the current answer file, press [Enter].

■ To save to a different answer file, press [Tab] to move to the Files box. Using the arrow keys, highlight the desired filename and [Enter] to select or point and click using a mouse.

Note: You may also save to an answer file by directly typing an eight-character filename.

If you select *NO* to Save Answers, Home Lawyer will display the File Menu.

Using Your Saved Answers

Home Lawyer lets you save your answers when a document is completed. The document can be re-created using those answers without re-typing information. You may use an answer set with any document. Related answers are automatically filled in to assist you in completing the document.

■   To prepare a document using your saved answers, highlight the document title from the Documents Menu and [Enter].

Home Lawyer automatically checks to see if a set of answers for any document exists. When one exists, a prompt appears.

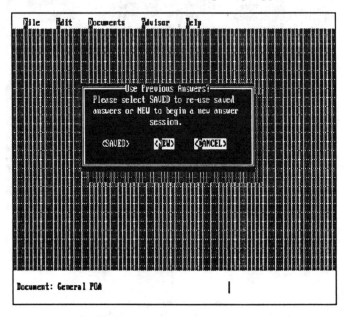

■   Use the arrow keys to highlight the desired option and [Enter] or point and click using a mouse.

Select *YES* to use the saved answers to complete the document.

Select *NO* to ignore the saved answers and enter new ones.

Select *CANCEL* to return to the Main Menu

If you select YES, the following Menu appears.

Select Answers

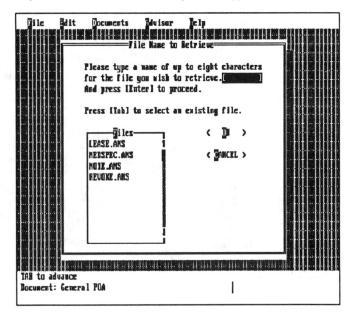

■ To select an existing answer file, press [Tab] to move to the Files box. Using the arrow keys, highlight the desired filename and [Enter] to select or point and click using a mouse.

Note: You may also select an answer file by directly typing the filename (e.g., MYWILL).

If you select NO, Home Lawyer will display the first Question and Answer Screen. The Response Area will be blank, ready for you to type new answers.

File Menu

■ To select the File Menu, press [Alt-F] or point and click using a mouse.

The File Menu contains the following options:

File Menu

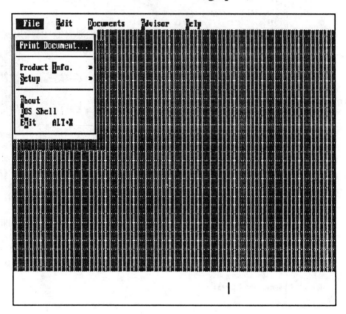

■ To select an option, use the arrow keys to highlight and [Enter] or point and click using a mouse.

Hint: You may also select an option by typing the highlighted letter of the menu item (e.g., **P** to Print).

Print Document

You can print the document immediately or save it as a file. Saving a document in a file lets you examine or format it using a word processor or text editor. You can also use this feature if you want to print another copy later.

Note: To print a document, it must have been selected. (See *Selecting a Document*.)

■ Press [Alt-F] to display the File Menu.

■ Highlight Print Document and [Enter].

The following options appear:

Print Menu

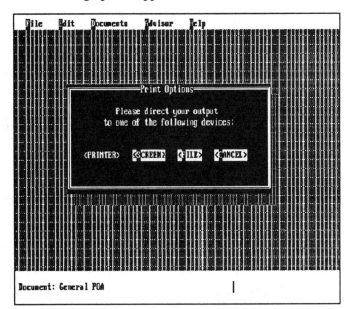

■ Use the arrow keys or press [Tab] to highlight the desired option and [Enter] or point and click using a mouse.

Select *PRINTER* to direct the output to your local printer.

Select *SCREEN* to view the assembled document on your screen.

Select *FILE* to save the assembled document to a file.

Select *CANCEL* to quit.

Printing to a Printer

■ Make sure your printer is turned on and ready to print.

■ Using your arrow keys, highlight < OK > and [Enter] to print the document.

Note: You may cancel print at any time. Press [Tab] to highlight <CANCEL> and [Enter].

Print Document to Screen

■ Use the up and down arrow keys to scroll through the document line by line.

■ Use the [PgUp] and [PgDn] keys to move through the document one screen at a time.

■ Press [Home] and [End] to quickly move to the beginning or end of the assembled document.

■ [Esc] to quit.

Printing to a File

After selecting *FILE*, the following Menu appears:

Print to File

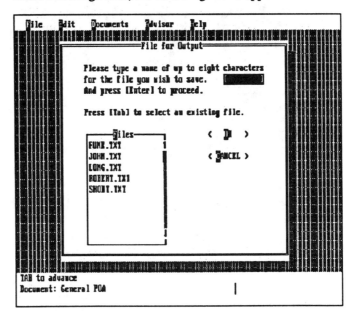

- Enter a valid DOS filename up to 8 characters and [Enter] or point and click on < OK > using a mouse.

- To select an existing file, press [Tab] to move to the Files box. Using the arrow keys, highlight the desired filename and [Enter] to select or point and click using a mouse.

If the filename you entered already exists, a prompt is displayed.

File Overwrite

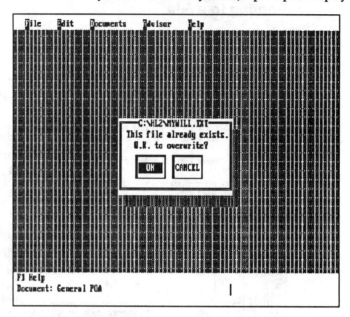

■ Highlight < OK > to overwrite, <CANCEL> to quit.

■ Press [Enter].

The following screen appears:

File Type Options

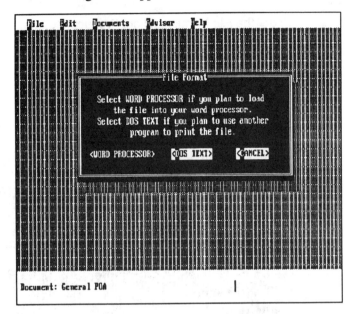

■ Use the arrow keys or [Tab] to highlight the desired option and [Enter] or point and click using a mouse.

Select *WORD PROCESSOR* if you plan to format and print the file using a word processor.

Select *DOS TEXT* if you plan to print using the DOS PRINT command or other similar utility.

The file is stored in standard text file format (ASCII). You can format or print the document using any word processor or text editor.

CAUTION: Do not make any modifications to the language of the document. Use your word processor or text editor only to format (e.g., margins, fonts, etc.) or print the document. Modifying the language may invalidate the document.

Product Information

■ Under the File Menu, highlight Product Info and [Enter] or point and click using a mouse.

The following options appear:

Product Information Options

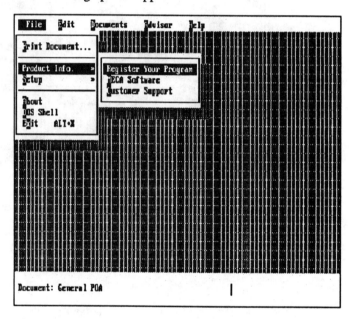

Register Your Program automatically prints a completed registration form using information entered in the User Profile (see *User Profile*).

MECA Software contains useful information about additional software programs available from **MECA** Software, Inc.

Customer Support describes our technical support policies and how to obtain the best service for your needs.

Register Your Program

If you have not yet registered your program, this option will automatically print out a registration form. Once printed, mail the form to the address indicated on the form.

Note: The program uses the User Profile information as a guide in printing the form. Be sure to fill out your User Profile before selecting this option. See *User Profile*.

MECA Software

This option will display a list of available software programs from MECA containing useful information about each product.

■ Using the arrow keys, highlight the desired software title and [Enter] or point and click using a mouse.

Customer Support

Customer Support describes our technical support policies and how to obtain the best service for your needs.

It includes a description of the type of support available including phone numbers and hours of operation.

Setup

- Under the File Menu, highlight Setup and [Enter] or point and
click using a mouse to display the following options:

Setup Options

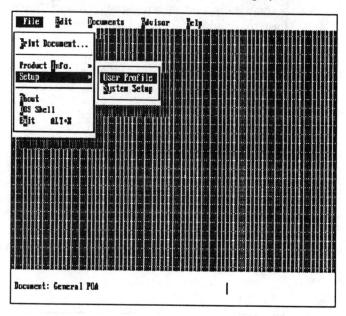

Select *User Profile* to enter personal information such as your name,
address and telephone number.

Select *System Setup* to enter printer and word processing setup
information.

User Profile

User Profile allows you to enter personal information such as your
name, address and phone number. This information is used to
complete an electronic registration form.

In addition, the data automatically appears during the Question and
Answer session to assist you in completing a document.

After selecting *User Profile*, the following screen appears:

User Profile

```
 File    Edit    Documents    Advisor    Help

                          User Profile

   Full name: Zane              R.  Thorogood

   Address 1: 2816 Temple of the Sun Highway

   Address 2:

       City: San Fernando        State: CA      Zip: 11092-0929

      Phone: (203) 028-2320 Social Security #: 023-98-2023


              < OK >                    <CANCEL>



 TAB to advance
 Document: General POA
```

■ Use [Tab] or the down arrow key to move to the next entry field.

■ Use [Shift-Tab] or the up arrow key to move back to the previous entry field.

■ Highlight <OK> using the [Tab] or arrow keys and press [Enter] or point and click using a mouse to quit and save your entries.

■ Press [Esc] or select <CANCEL> to quit and discard your answers.

Note: Be sure to update this screen as your personal data changes.

System Setup

After selecting System Setup, the following screen appears:

System Setup

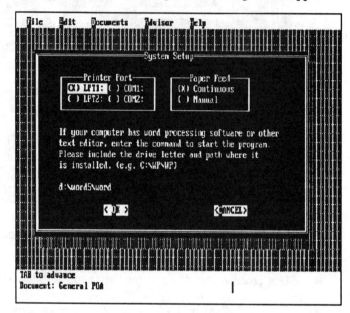

- Use the arrow keys to move the "X" to the correct printer port for your system configuration. Press [Tab] to move to the next box.

- Use the arrow keys to move the "X" to the correct type of paper feed for your printer. If you have a paper tray or the paper is tractor fed, choose continuous. If you have to insert the paper by hand one sheet at a time, choose manual.

- Press [Tab] to move to the next field.

- Enter the full path and filename of your Word Processor (leave this blank if you do not use a word processor).

Note: Entering the word processing name and path allows you to immediately shell or execute your word processor from within Home Lawyer. See *Shell to WP*.

■ Highlight <OK> using the [Tab] or arrow keys and [Enter] or point and click using a mouse to quit and save your entries.

■ Press [Esc] or select <CANCEL> to quit and discard your answers.

About

This option displays licensing information about Home Lawyer and available memory from within the program.

■ Press [Enter] or point and click on <OK> using a mouse to clear the screen.

DOS Shell This option will automatically shell to a DOS prompt. From there, you may enter and execute DOS commands.

■ Type EXIT and [Enter] to return to Home Lawyer.

Exit This option will exit Home Lawyer. You can exit from anywhere in the program.

■ Highlight Exit using the arrow keys and [Enter] or point and click using a mouse.

■ Type [Alt-X] at any time to exit the program.

■ Press [Enter] to confirm.

Edit Menu

■ To select the Edit Menu, press [Alt-E] or point and click using a mouse.

The Edit Menu contains the following options:

Edit Menu

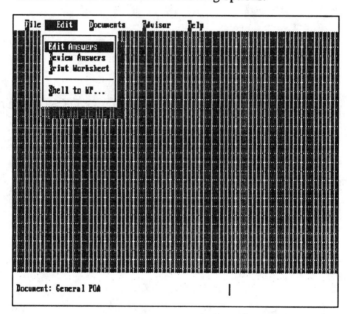

■ To select an option, use the arrow keys to highlight and [Enter] or point and click using a mouse.

Hint: You may also select an option by typing the shaded letter of the menu item (e.g., P to Print).

Edit Answers

Edit Answers allows you to change one or more entries after completing a Question and Answer session for a document.

Note: Before you can edit your answers, a document must have been selected and answers entered. See *Documents Menu* and *Question and Answer Session*.

■ Use the arrow keys or type "E" to highlight Edit Answers and [Enter] or point and click using a mouse.

The Question and Answer screen will be displayed starting at the first question for the selected document. Your first answer appears in the Response Area.

■ Use the editing keys to make changes or corrections. (See *Editing Key Summary*.)

■ [Alt-N], [Enter] or [F10] moves you forward through the questions.

■ [Alt-P] or [F9] moves you to the previous question.

■ After making the necessary changes, press [Esc] to save your answers. (See *Saving Your Answers*.)

Note: Changing a Yes/No or multiple choice answer may result in a different series of questions being asked.

Review Answers

You can check your answers to make sure everything is entered correctly.

■ From the Edit Menu, highlight Review Answers using the arrow keys and [Enter] or point and click using a mouse.

The Review Answer screen displays.

- Use [PgDn] to see the rest of the information if the answers continue beyond the first screen.

- [Esc] to return to the Edit Menu.

    Note: You cannot change answers using this option. If you want to change or correct an answer, select Edit Answers from the Edit Menu. (See *Edit Answers*.)

Print Worksheets

The worksheet option prints a list of the questions used with a particular document. Use the worksheet as a guide when collecting information.

- At the Home Lawyer Main Menu, highlight the desired document title and [Enter] to select it.

- At the Question and Answer screen, press [Alt-E] to display the Edit Menu.

- Using the arrow keys, highlight Print Worksheet. Press [Enter].

The following message appears.

Worksheet Options

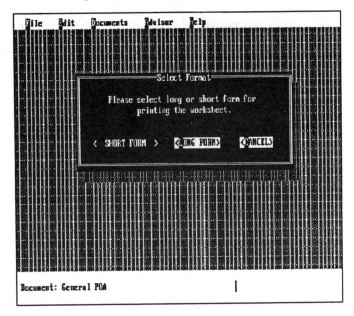

Select *SHORT FORM* to print just your answers.

Select *LONG FORM* to print the question as well as your answers.

Select *CANCEL* to return to the Main Menu.

■ Using your arrow keys, highlight your selection.

The following print options appears.

Print Options

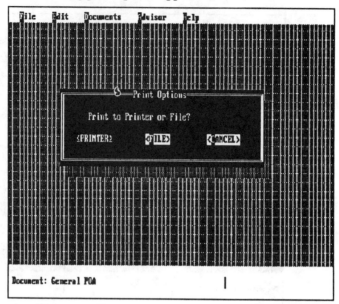

- Make sure your printer is turned on and ready to print.

- Using your arrow keys, highlight your selection and [Enter].

The following print message appears.

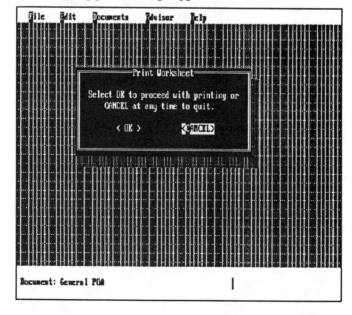

■ Highlight < OK > and [Enter] to print the worksheet.

When the worksheet has been printed, Home Lawyer will return to the Question and Answer Screen.

■ Continue to answer the questions or press [Esc] to return to the Main Menu.

Hint: You can print a worksheet at any time during a Question and Answer session. Write additional information on the worksheet and use that as a typing guide to complete document preparation.

Shell to WP   This option will automatically shell or execute a word processing program entered under System Setup. (See *System Setup*.)

■ From the Edit Menu, highlight Shell to WP using the arrow keys and [Enter] or point and click using a mouse.

When you exit your word processor, you will automatically return to the Home Lawyer Main Menu.

Note: If your word processing program does not properly execute, check your System Setup to make sure the name and path of your word processor is correctly identified. Home Lawyer must know the *path* and *name* of the executable (e.g., C:\WP\WP).

Advisor Menu

■   To select the Advisor Menu, press [Alt-A] or point and click using
   a mouse.

The following list of options appear:

Advisor Menu

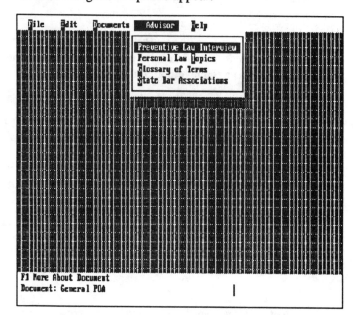

■   To select an option, use the arrow keys to highlight and [Enter] or
   point and click using a mouse.

Hint: You may also select an option by typing the shaded letter of
the menu item (e.g., P to Print).

Select *Preventive Law Interview* to generate a personalized report referring you to useful legal information in Home Lawyer relevant to your needs.

Select *Personal Law Topics* to review important legal topics ranging from *Wills and Trusts* to *Going to Court*.

Select *Glossary of Terms* to display an alphabetized list of terms and their definitions.

Select *State Bar Associations* to display the address and phone number for your State Bar Association.

Preventive Law Interview

The Preventive Law Interview leads you through a series of questions and generates a personalized report directing you to areas of interest in the Home Lawyer program.

■ From the Advisor Menu, highlight Preventive Law Interview using the arrow keys and [Enter] or point and click using a mouse.

The Question and Answer screen appears ready to enter data. For more information see *Question and Answer Session*.

Personal Law Topics

■ From the Advisor Menu, highlight Personal Law Topics using the arrow keys and [Enter] or point and click using a mouse.

An outline of twelve topics will appear.

Personal Law Topics

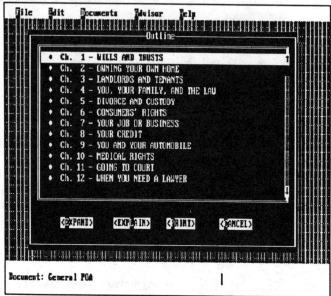

You can Expand a topic into subtopics, receive an explanation or description of the topic, print the topic or cancel to the top line menu.

Expand

To Expand a topic, use the arrow keys to highlight the topic of your choice, or point and click using a mouse. Press [Alt-E] to Expand the selected topic or point and click on <EXPAND> using a mouse.

The topic will expand to display its subtopics.

Topics with Subtopics Displayed

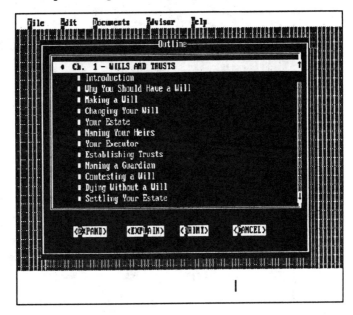

Hint: Pressing [Enter] will expand a topic. Pressing [Enter] again will close the topic.

Explain

Use EXPLAIN to get additional information on a topic.

■ Use the arrow keys to highlight a topic or point and click using a mouse.

■ Once the correct topic is highlighted, press [Alt-L] or point and click on <EXPLAIN> using a mouse.

A window containing additional text on the chosen topic appears.

Personal Law Topic Text

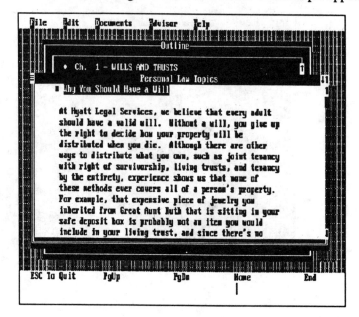

- Use the [PgUp] and [PgDn] keys to review the text for the selected topic.

- [Esc] to close the window.

- [Esc] once more to clear the screen and quit to the Main Menu.

Print

Use Print to output the information for the selected topic to a printer or a file.

- Using the arrow keys, highlight a topic or point and click using a mouse.

- Once the correct topic is highlighted, press [Alt-P] or point and click on <PRINT> using a mouse.

Cancel

■ To exit Personal Law Topics, type [Alt-C] and [Enter] or point and click on <CANCEL> using a mouse.

Glossary of Terms

Glossary of Terms displays an alphabetized list of legal terms and their definitions.

■ From the Advisor Menu, highlight Glossary of Terms using the arrow keys and [Enter] or point and click using a mouse.

A list of legal terms appears.

Legal Terms Index

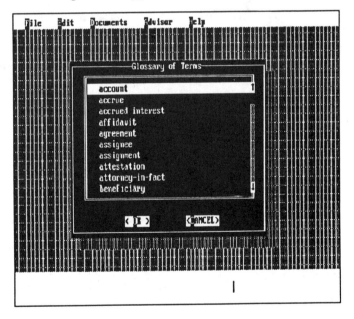

■ Using the arrow keys, highlight the term you want defined and [Enter] or point and click on <OK> using a mouse.

Hint: Type the first letter of a word to quickly jump to that section of the list. Use [End] to quickly move to the end of the list. Use [Home] to quickly move to the beginning of the list.

The definition window appears.

Legal Term Definitions

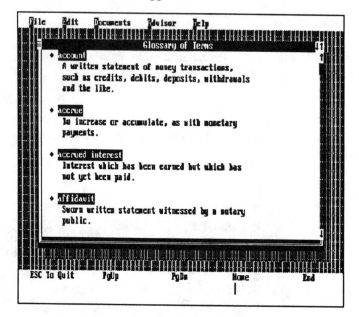

■   Use the arrow keys to scroll through the definitions.

■   [Esc] to return to the alphabetical listing.

■   [Esc] once more to clear the screen and return to the Main Menu.

State Bar Associations

■   From the Advisor Menu, highlight State Bar Associations using the arrow keys and [Enter] or point and click using a mouse.

A list of states in alphabetical order appears.

■   Select your state using the arrow keys and [Enter] or point and click using a mouse.

Your State Bar Association address and telephone number appears.

State Bar Association
Information

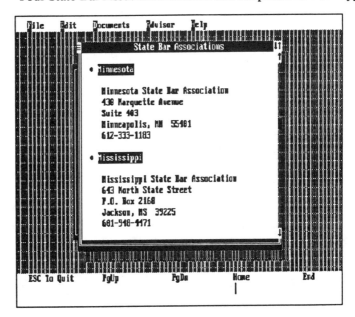

■   [Esc] to return to the alphabetical listing.

■   [Esc] once more to clear the screen and return to the Main Menu.

Personal Law Interview

Document Summary

At Hyatt Legal Services, we think it's important to ask our clients some basic questions during their first office visit. The answers to these questions help our attorneys identify the areas where our services can be useful, and let us provide helpful advice about areas our clients otherwise might not have considered.

We're firm believers in the practice of preventive law. That means evaluating your legal needs before a problem arises. Practicing preventive law saves our clients unnecessary worry and expense, and can even help to alleviate the burdens faced by our court system.

The following screens contain the kinds of questions our attorneys would ask you during an initial consultation at one of our offices. Once you've answered them, Home Lawyer analyzes your responses and provides a Preventive Law Report to identify the documents and topics in this program that may be of interest to you.

Questions and Comments

Legal Name

Please enter your full legal name.

[Example: Jonathan A. Doe]

Comment: Do not use any nicknames or abbreviations. The name must be the legal name, not the social name.

User Age

Are you over 55 years of age?

( ) YES
( ) NO

Comment: Select "YES" if you are over the age of 55. Otherwise, select "NO".

Marital Status   **Enter your marital status.**

( ) Married
( ) Unmarried

Comment: Select "Married" if you are married or separated. Select "Unmarried" if you are single, divorced or widowed.

Minor Child   **Are any of your child(ren) under the age of 18?**

( ) YES
( ) NO

Comment: Select "NO" if you have no children. Press [Enter] or <NEXT> to move to the next question.

Last Will   **Do you have a Last Will and Testament?**

( ) YES
( ) NO

Comment: Select "YES" if your Will was written or reviewed by you during the past 12 months. Otherwise, select "NO".

Living Will   **Do you have a current Living Will?**

( ) YES
( ) NO

Comment: Select "YES" if your Living Will was written or reviewed by you in the past 12 months. Otherwise, select "NO".

Own or Rent   **Do you own your home, or do you rent?**

( ) Own
( ) Rent

Comment: If you own a single family home or condominium, or if you belong to a cooperative, select "Own". Otherwise select "Rent".

Residential Property   **Do you own residential property that you rent to others?**

( ) YES
( ) NO

Comment: Select "YES" if you own a house or condominium which you rent to tenants for use as their residence.

Buy a Home	**Are you considering purchasing a home in the next 6 months?**

( ) YES
( ) NO

Comment: Select "YES" or "NO".

Own a Car	**Do you own or lease an automobile?**

( ) YES
( ) NO

Comment: Select "YES" if you own or lease your car. Otherwise, select "NO".

Mail Order	**Do you ever purchase items by mail, or over the telephone?**

( ) YES
( ) NO

Comment: Select "YES" if you do. Otherwise, select "NO".

Employment	**Are you employed by another, or do you own your own business?**

( ) Employed by another
( ) Own my own business

Comment: Make the desired selection and press [Enter] or <NEXT> to continue.

Starting a Business	**Are you considering starting your own business in the next year?**

( ) YES
( ) NO

Comment: Make the desired selection and press [Enter] or <NEXT> to continue.

Employer	**Do you employ others in your business?**

( ) YES
( ) NO

Comment: Select "YES" even if you have only one other employee. Otherwise, select "NO".

Income   **Please enter your average gross annual income.**

( ) $0-$45,000
( ) $45,000 or More

Comment: Be sure to consider all your income, including salaries and commissions, interest, alimony, and support payments.

Lend Money   **Have you loaned, or considered lending money to another person?**

( ) YES
( ) NO

Comment: Make the desired selection and press [Enter] or <NEXT> to continue.

Refused Credit   **Have you been refused credit during the past 30 days?**

( ) YES
( ) NO

Comment: Select "YES" if you've been turned down for a loan from a bank, savings and loan, credit card company, credit union or loan company. Otherwise, select "NO".

Parent   **Do you have living parents over the age of 60?**

( ) YES
( ) NO

Comment: Make the desired selection and press [Enter] or <NEXT> to move to the next question.

Attorney   **Do you have an attorney?**

( ) YES
( ) NO

Comment: Select "YES" if you have visited an attorney in the past year or if you have an attorney who provides assistance on a regular basis.

Date today   **Enter the date today.**

[Example: 11/2/91]

Comment: Enter the month, date, and year.

Personal Law Topics

Home Lawyer's Personal Law Topics contains information about the law and its impact on many areas of your life, from home ownership to estate planning, from family law to buying and selling an automobile.

The following is a list of chapters and related topics. The reference material for each topic is available on-line under the *Advisor* menu (see *Personal Law Topics* under the *Advisor Menu* section in Chapter 3).

Chapter 1 -- Wills and Trusts

Introduction

In this chapter, we'll look at the most important legal document a person can have, the Last Will and Testament. We'll also talk about establishing a support trust for your children, and we'll discuss some ways to minimize probate costs.

- Why You Should Have a Will
- Making a Will
- Changing Your Will
- Your Estate
- Naming Your Heirs
- Your Executor
- Establishing Trusts
- Naming a Guardian
- Contesting a Will
- Dying Without a Will
- Settling Your Estate
- How To Avoid Probate
- Funerals and Burials
- Living Wills

Chapter 2 --
Owning Your
Own Home

Introduction

For most people, the purchase of a home is the biggest investment they'll ever make. Unlike most other investments, there is a lot of emotion attached to the purchase of a home. While we can't help you if you're overcome by love at first sight for that little cottage by the sea (probably nobody can), we can show you some of the legal issues surrounding buying and selling a home.

This chapter also explores the rights and responsibilities that come with home ownership. If you're a renter, or if you're thinking about becoming a landlord, we suggest you look at the chapter entitled Landlords and Tenants for information.

- **Buying and Selling a Home**
- **Being a Homeowner**

Chapter 3 --
Landlords and
Tenants

Introduction

At one time or another, nearly all of us will live in a rental home or apartment. Thousands of other Americans act as landlords, leasing one or more units to renters. In this chapter, we'll take a brief look at the rights and responsibilities of both landlords and tenants, and discuss some of the laws affecting the landlord-tenant relationship.

- **Leasing Residential Property**
- **Tenants' Rights**
- **Landlords' Rights**
- **Security Deposits**
- **Discrimination**
- **Evictions**

Chapter 4 --
You, Your
Family, and the
Law

Introduction

Not so many years ago, the law considered a man's wife and children as little better than property, and he was free to treat them accordingly. As with so many areas of our society, the laws surrounding the relationships of husband and wife and parent and child have changed significantly over the past several decades. In this chapter, we'll look at the laws that relate to family life and relationships. We'll explore the laws about marriage and some of the modern alternatives to marriage, and we'll examine the rights of children and the elderly.

- **Marriage**
- **Prenuptial Agreements**
- **Unmarried Couples, Unwed Parents**
- **Adoption**
- **Caring for a Parent**

Chapter 5 --
Divorce and
Custody

Introduction

Probably no area of the law has undergone as much change in the past two decades as divorce law. Few areas of the law affect so many people. According to statistics, about 50% of all marriages in this country will end in divorce, and nearly two million Americans will divorce this year. In this chapter, we'll look at some of the issues surrounding the dissolution of a marriage, as well as the continuing responsibilities and rights divorced parents have in regard to their children.

- **Types of Divorce**
- **The Divorce Process**
- **Dividing Your Property**
- **Child Support**
- **Spousal Support**
- **Child Custody and Visitation Rights**

Chapter 6 --
Consumers'
Rights

Introduction

At one time, consumers' rights could just about be summed up by the phrase "let the buyer beware." Today, consumers are afforded much greater legal protection from shady merchants and shoddy merchandise. And yet thousands of consumers this year will be victimized despite the state and federal laws designed to protect them. In this chapter, we'll examine your rights as a consumer and provide some information to help you avoid a bad deal, or find help if you've already made one.

- **Consumer Contracts**
- **Buying by Mail**
- **Telephone Sales and Scams**
- **Door-to-Door Sales**
- **Defective and Unsafe Merchandise**
- **When You Have A Complaint**
- **For More Information**

Chapter 7 --
Your Job or
Business

Introduction

Whether you work for someone else or own your own business, you are affected by the law in many ways. In this chapter, we will look at just a few of the legal issues surrounding employment and business ownership. We will also discuss some of the legal ramifications of layoffs, terminations, and injuries suffered on the job.

- **Applying for a Job**
- **Employee Benefits**
- **Job Discrimination**
- **Workers' Compensation**
- **Owning Your Own Business**

Chapter 8 --
Your Credit

Introduction

Almost no one would argue that Americans live in a credit-based society. Consumer loans, credit cards, home mortgages, and other kinds of financing arrangements allow us to purchase many items which cost more than we have readily available in cash. In this chapter, we will look at the ways in which you can obtain credit and keep your credit record clean, and discuss some of the steps you can take if your debts do become a problem.

- **Establishing Credit**
- **Selecting a Credit Card**
- **Personal Loans**
- **Consumer Credit Protection**
- **Payment Problems**
- **Bankruptcy and Its Alternatives**

Chapter 9 --
You and Your
Automobile

Introduction

With the average price of a new car now well in excess of $15,000, it pays to be a well-informed car purchaser. In this chapter, we will look at the advantages and disadvantages to buying versus leasing an automobile, and make some comparisons between purchasing a new vehicle and one that is pre-owned. (Remember when they were called used?) We will also look at automobile warranties and repairs, insurance requirements, drunk driving laws, and what you should do if you are ever involved in an automobile accident.

- **Buying A New Car**
- **Leasing a Car**
- **Buying or Selling A Used Car**
- **Car Warranties**
- **Lemon Laws**
- **Automobile Insurance**
- **Drinking And Driving**
- **Automobile Accidents**

Chapter 10 --
Medical Rights

Introduction

The rapid advances in medical technology over the past several decades have also led to significant new areas of interaction between the law and medicine. In this chapter, we will look at some of the traditional rights of persons receiving medical treatment, and we will also examine some of the new issues related to the so-called "right to die."

- **Your Rights As a Patient**
- **Consenting to Medical Treatment**
- **Medical Malpractice**
- **The Right to Die**
- **The Right to Life**

Chapter 11 --
Going to Court

Introduction

Although Home Lawyer is designed to provide legal documents that clearly state your rights and responsibilities and help keep you out of the courtroom, the day may come when you need to participate in a legal proceeding as a plaintiff, defendant, witness, or perhaps as a juror. In this chapter, we will take a brief look at the judicial system, your role as a witness, and the function of a juror. We will also examine small claims court procedures and the way to present a small claims case.

- **Our Judicial System**
- **Civil Court Procedures**
- **Being A Witness**
- **Being A Juror**
- **Small Claims Court**
- **Going to Court - Conclusion**

Chapter 12 --
When You
Need A Lawyer

Introduction

While Home Lawyer contains the legal documents people use most often, no computer program can address all the legal issues a person may face. In some cases, the advice and assistance of an attorney will be invaluable in helping to spot potential legal problems or in guiding you toward the best decision regarding your family, property, business or career. The personalized help of an attorney can go far beyond what even the best computer program can do. You should consult with an attorney when:

- You need help in selecting the document that is right for your situation.

- You are asked to sign any document you do not fully understand or with which you do not agree.

- You need access to the court system to assert your rights or to defend yourself against the claims of another.

- Your estate is in excess of $600,000 or you need assistance with planning your estate.

- You need guidance in filing papers or recording legal documents.

- You are charged with any criminal violation or served with a civil lawsuit.

- You need advice or further explanation about any of the language contained in Home Lawyer's documents.

- **Finding the Right Lawyer**
- **Legal Fees and Expenses**
- **Lawyers' Ethics**

Estate Planning Worksheet

Document Summary

The federal government assesses estate taxes on estates valued at over $600,000, although you can leave your entire estate to a spouse without incurring any estate tax. Federal estate taxes can be substantial, ranging from 38% to 55% of the value of your estate in excess of $600,000.

For tax purposes, the IRS considers everything you own at the time of your death, no matter what form that ownership takes. So even though you can avoid probate of some assets, such as life insurance proceeds payable to a named beneficiary and property held in joint tenancy, you can't avoid estate taxes on them.

The Estate Planning Worksheet takes you through a list of assets and asks you to assign a value to them. While you don't have to figure values down to the penny, you should try to be as accurate as possible. Remember to include your share of any property held in joint tenancy or tenancy in common.

When you're finished, you may be surprised at the value of your estate. If the total is much higher than you thought, even if it doesn't quite reach the $600,000 threshold, you may want to consider getting some professional assistance with planning techniques that can help to reduce the taxes on your estate.

Questions and Comments

Estate Worksheet

This Estate Planning Worksheet asks you to enter the amount in dollars ($) of the value of things you own, and then the amount of debt you owe. When asked for the amount you own or the value of an item or asset, enter the full value without deduction for any amounts owed for that item.

Comment: When complete, review the printed Worksheet as an estimate of your total net worth for purposes of Estate Planning.

Cash Amount

Enter the amount of cash you own. This includes cash you hold in checking and passbook savings accounts at banks, savings and loans, and credit unions, as well as cash on hand at home.

[Example: 3,550.00]

Comment: Enter the amount of immediately available cash.

Note: The program automatically adds commas where necessary.

Certificates

Enter the value of any Certificates of Deposit or Money Market Certificates you own.

[Example: 13,500.00]

Note: The program automatically adds commas where necessary.

Comment: Include the value of any certificates which provide a penalty for early withdrawal.

Stocks and Bonds	**Enter the value of any stocks and bonds you own. Include the value of stock held for you through any employee ownership plan administered by your employer.**

[Example: 6,000.00]

Note: The program automatically adds commas where necessary.

Comment: If you operate a business structured as a corporation, include the value of your stock here.

Retirement Benefits	**Enter the value of any IRA, Keogh, annuity, pension, or other retirement benefit plan.**

[Example: 8,000.00]

Note: The program automatically adds commas where necessary.

Comment: Enter the current value of these assets, not their expected value on retirement.

Business Value	**If you operate a business as a sole proprietorship or as a partnership, enter the current value of your interest in the business. Be sure to count only your interest in the business.**

[Example: 75,000.00]

Note: The program automatically adds commas where necessary.

Comment: If your business is structured as a corporation, the value of your stock should have been entered in Question 4 *Stocks and Bonds*; do not include it here.

Royalty Income	**Enter royalty payments which you receive from publications, patents, etc.**

[Example: 2,300.00]

Note: The program automatically adds commas where necessary.

Comment: Enter estimated annual value of any royalties paid to you by publishers, manufacturers, or others.

Include the value of any compensation paid to you by publishers and manufacturer for use of copyrights or patents you hold, as well as compensation you receive from oil, gas, or other natural resource companies.

Debts Owed You

Enter any debts owed to you by others.

[Example: 23,000.00]

Note: The program automatically adds commas where necessary.

Comment: Enter the principal amount owed to you, as well as any interest accrued but unpaid as of today.

Real Estate

Enter the full market value of any real estate you own. The program automatically adds commas where necessary.

[Example: 98,000.00]

Note: Do not deduct the amount of any mortgage or other loans secured by this property.

Comment: Include your share of the market value of your home, as well as the market value of your interest in vacation property, commercial property, or undeveloped land.

Life Insurance

Enter the value of any life insurance policies.

[Example: 50,000.00]

Note: The program automatically adds commas where necessary.

Comment: Do not include any cash surrender value, but only the benefit payable upon your death. Remember to include any group life policy provided by your employer.

Miscellaneous   **Enter the value of all your other property.**

[Example: 36,000.00]

Note: The program automatically adds commas where necessary.

Comment: Include such items as automobiles, boats and trailers, furniture, jewelry, antiques and so on.

Mortgage   **Enter the amount of any mortgage debt you owe (principal only).**

[Example: 43,000.00]

Note: The program automatically adds commas where necessary.

Comment: Include the unpaid balance of any mortgages, second mortgages, or home equity loans which you owe on your home or other real estate.

Loans   **Enter the amount of any automobile loans or other consumer loans you owe.**

[Example: 3,200.00]

Note: The program automatically adds commas where necessary.

Comment: Include the unpaid balance of all fixed payment loans such as consumer loans, student loans and automobile or recreational vehicle loans.

Credit Card Debt   **Enter the amount of credit card debt you owe.**

[Example: 750.00]

Note: The program automatically adds commas where necessary.

Comment: Enter the current balance owed on bank credit cards, travel and entertainment cards, department store charge accounts and gasoline credit cards.

**Miscellaneous
Debt**

Enter the amount of any miscellaneous debts you owe.

[Example: 350.00]

*Note: The program automatically adds commas where
necessary.*

Comment: Include all other debts you owe, such as promissory
notes, amounts owed to family members, and so on.

Sample Document[1]

ESTATE PLANNING WORKSHEET

ASSETS

Cash on Hand	$2,500.00
Certificates of Deposit	$5,000.00
Stocks and Bonds	$5,000.00
IRA, Keogh, Annuity, Retirement Benefits	$0.00
Sole Proprietor, Partnership Value	$0.00
Debts Owed to You	$0.00
Real Estate	$95,000.00
Life Insurance	$75,000.00
Royalty Income	$0.00
Miscellaneous	$25,000.00
Total Assets	**$207,500.00**

LIABILITIES

Mortgages	$60,000.00
Auto and Consumer Loans	$16,000.00
Credit Card Debt	$4,500.00
Miscellaneous Debt	$2,000.00
Total Liabilities	**$82,500.00**
NET VALUE OF YOUR ESTATE	**$125,000.00**

[1] The sample document has been prepared and formatted for illustration purposes only. The actual document will print using the standard type style of your printer and the number of lines per page may differ.

Last Will and Testament

Document Summary

If you are over the age of 18, you should prepare a Last Will and Testament. A will is important whether or not you have children, or whether or not you own property. A will helps protect those you care about.

It spells out your wishes so that your family members don't have to try to make decisions they feel uncomfortable with. It will save them the added grief at a time when they need it the least.

Generally, any person who is over the age of 18 (19 in Wyoming) and who is of sound mind can make a valid will. A person is considered of sound mind if he or she knows the nature of the property owned, the consequences of disposing of that property, and makes the will voluntarily and free of any undue influence or duress imposed by someone else.

Your Last Will and Testament contains your instructions regarding the disposition of your property after your death.

If you die without leaving a will, the laws of your state will determine what happens to your property. If you are married with children, your surviving spouse may receive only one-third to one-half of your property. Your children will receive the rest.

If you are married but have no children, your surviving spouse may receive anywhere from one-third of your estate to all of your estate, depending on state law. In states where your surviving spouse receives less than your entire estate, the other portion is divided among your surviving parents, brothers and sisters, and their descendants.

If you have no spouse but leave children, they will share your estate, and if a child of yours has died but left children, they will also receive a portion of your estate. If you have no spouse or children who survive you, other relatives will divide the property you leave behind.

Home Lawyer's Last Will and Testament lets you write a simple will. You may leave up to 30 specific gifts of property to anyone you choose. You may leave the rest of your property (called your residuary estate) to whomever you choose. If you are married, you should keep in mind that state laws may prevent you from disinheriting your surviving spouse. Consult with an attorney for information about the law in your state.

Keep in mind that certain kinds of property cannot be disposed of in a will. For example, property owned as "Joint Tenants with Right of Survivorship," automatically goes to the other joint tenant when you die. Life insurance and pension benefits usually go to someone you name as a beneficiary in your insurance policy or pension documents.

Because Home Lawyer's Last Will and Testament is designed to be a simple will, you should not use it if your net estate (the value of what you own minus any debts you owe) exceeds $600,000. Because of certain requirements in Louisiana state law, this will is not valid in Louisiana. Contact an attorney to help you prepare a will if you live in Louisiana.

In order for your Last Will and Testament to be valid it must be properly executed. Information on executing your Will can be found below under *Special Considerations*. Instructions on executing your Will print automatically when you print your completed Last Will and Testament.

Special Considerations

Before your Last Will and Testament becomes valid, it must be properly executed. Although state laws vary, these steps should enable you to make your Last Will and Testament valid in your state (except Louisiana).

1. You will need three witnesses. You should sign your Will in front of the three of them at the same time. As you sign it, tell them that this document is your Last Will and Testament and that you are asking them to sign it as witnesses. (You may also want to initial each page to prevent anyone from making alterations to your Will. If you do, initial it at the bottom of each page, and have your Witnesses put their initials next to yours.) You do not have to reveal the contents of your Will to your Witnesses.

2. Have the Witnesses sign on the appropriate lines. You must watch each Witness sign, and each of them must watch the others sign.

3. In most states, the Affidavit that printed with your Will allows your Executor to begin the probate of your estate without having to call your Witnesses to court to prove that your Will is really your Will. (This is called "proving" the Will; the affidavit is called a "self-proving" affidavit.)

To make your Will self-proving, you should read and sign the affidavit on the line indicated. Your Witnesses should read the affidavit and sign it in your presence, in the presence of each other, and in the presence of a notary public.

While certain states do not recognize self-proving affidavits, having one anyway will not affect your Will's validity. Neither will not having one in states that honor them. The choice is yours.

Your Witnesses should be at least 21 years old, and they should not include anyone who will receive any of your property under your Will.

DO NOT sign any copies of your Will, or make copies of your signed Will. Sign only the original, using the procedure outlined above.

DO NOT make any changes, alterations or additions to your Will once it is printed. If you need to make a change, go back to the program and print a new document. Be sure to destroy the incorrect Will immediately, so there is no confusion later about which version is the correct one.

Keep the executed original of your Will in a safe place. A fireproof file box or home safe is usually better than a bank safety deposit box, since some states seal the box on your death. This could delay the probate of your estate. Wherever you keep your executed Will, be sure to tell someone you trust (for example, your Executor) where it can be found in the event of your death. Attaching a list of your assets (insurance policy numbers, bank account information, etc.) will help your Executor carry out your wishes with a minimum of delay.

Questions and Comments

Note: The following describes every question for the Last Will and Testament. However, during the Question and Answer session, the program will display only those questions relevant to your personal situation.

Legal Name   **Please enter your full legal name.**

[Example: Jonathan A. Doe]

Comment: Do not use any nicknames or abbreviations. The name must be your legal name, not your social name.

Use SSN?   **Do you want to include your social security number in your Will?**

Comment: Your social security number will help to positively identify this document as your Last Will and Testament. If you'd rather not use your social security number, select "NO".

SSN   **Enter your Social Security Number.**

[Example: 159-45-6789]

Comment: Double-check the number to make sure you have entered it correctly. It is very important to record the number accurately.

Male/Female   **Choose your gender.**

( ) Male
( ) Female

Comment: This choice controls gender replacement within the document.

City
: **Enter the name of the city where you live.**

  [Example: Chicago]

  Comment: Enter the name of the city, town, or village you live in, but don't use the name of a real estate subdivision. For example, if you live in the Blair Estate subdivision of Shaker, use Shaker.

State
: **Enter the state where you live.**

  [Example: IL]

  Comment: Use the two-letter abbreviation for your state.

Marital Status
: **Enter your marital status.**

  ( ) Married
  ( ) Unmarried

  Comment: Select "Married" if you are married or separated. Select "Unmarried" if you are single, divorced or widowed.

Spouse Name
: **Please enter your spouse's full legal name.**

  [Example: Mary B. Doe]

  Comment: Enter your spouse's full legal name, first name first, last name last. Please do not use nicknames or your spouse's social name. For example, use "Mary B. Doe" not "Mrs. John Doe."

Children
: **Do you have any children?**

  ( ) YES
  ( ) NO

  Comment: Select "YES" or "NO". Press [Enter] or select <NEXT> to move to the next question.

Number Children **How many living children do you have?**

[Example: 3]

Note: Home Lawyer allows up to 12 children.

Comment: Count all of your living children, including any children by a previous marriage, children born out of wedlock, and children you have legally adopted.

Child Names **Please enter the names of your child(ren).**

[Example: *James C. Doe*
               Jennifer D. Doe]

Comment: Again be sure not to use abbreviations or nicknames. If you have more than one child type each child's name on a separate line. Press [Enter] to move to the next line. Select <NEXT> to move to the next question.

Specific Bequest **Do you want to give specific items of your property or specific amounts of cash to any individual or organization?**

( ) YES
( ) NO

Comment: You may give specific gifts, also called "specific bequests", of personal property, real property, and specific amounts of cash to people or organizations.

Personal property are things such as jewelry, furniture, cars, stocks, etc.

Real property includes things such as houses, undeveloped real estate, condominiums, etc.

You can give personal property, real property or specific amounts of cash to people or organizations such as charities, fraternal organizations, etc.

How Many Bequests

Enter the number of specific gifts you want to make, up to 30.

[Example: 6]

Comment: Home Lawyer lets you make specific bequests to as many as 30 individuals or organizations. You may give each person or organization more than one gift.

Bequest Comment

When entering a specific gift, it is extremely important to clearly identify the gift as well as the person or organization who will receive it. You may enter an alternate recipient if your first named residuary beneficiary fails to survive you by 30 days. If you do not wish to name an alternate leave the field blank.

Comment: Please press [F1] for additional comments. Press [Enter] or select <NEXT> to continue.

When giving a specific gift, it is extremely important to clearly identify the gift as well as the person or organization who will receive it. Incomplete identification may mean that the gift will fail, and the item you wanted to give will pass into your residuary estate.

When entering a description of the specific gift you're making identify the item clearly and completely. For example, "my 1989 blue 4-door Toyota Camry, VIN 81J657823K," is much better than just "my car." If you're giving more than one gift to the same person or organization, separate the items with semi-colons, but do not use a period to end your entry.

Enter the name of the person or organization who will receive the gift. If the gift is to an individual, it's helpful to further identify the individual with a brief description of your relationship. For example, "my friend, Jennifer Stewart," or "my son, Harold Anderson." Please don't use nicknames or abbreviations.

If the gift is to an organization, be as specific as possible in naming it. For example, "the Halstead Street Shelter in Hometown," is much better than "the homeless shelter downtown."

Home Lawyer lets you name an alternate recipient for a specific gift if the first person or organization you name fails to survive you by 30 days. If you do not want to name an alternate recipient, the gift will become part of your residuary estate.

Gift One   **Enter a description of the gift you want to leave. Next, enter the name of the person or organization to receive it. Then, if you want to name an alternate recipient, enter that name.**

Note: This question will repeat for the number of specified bequests entered earlier.

Residuary Estate   **Most people who are married with children leave their residuary estate to their spouse. If their spouse fails to survive them, they leave their residuary estate in equal shares to their children. How do you want to leave your residuary estate?**

( ) Spouse then Children in Equal Shares
( ) Leave it in Another Manner

Comment: Your residuary estate is all the property left in your estate after you've made any specific gifts.

You must name a residuary beneficiary for your estate. While you can name any person or organization to receive your residuary estate, most married people will choose to leave their residuary estate to their spouse then children. Keep in mind that state laws will generally allow your spouse to receive a portion of your estate no matter how much you leave by Will.

How Many Residuaries   **How many persons or organizations do you want to receive your residuary estate?**

( ) One Residuary Beneficiary
( ) Two or more Residuary Beneficiaries

Comment: Your residuary estate is all the property left in your estate after you've made any specific gifts. You must name a residuary beneficiary for your estate.

Residuary Names   **Enter the name of the person(s) or organization(s) you want to receive your residuary estate. If you name more than one residuary beneficiary, enter each name on a separate line.**

[Example: my friend, Jack Smith]

Comment: It is helpful to precede the name of a residuary beneficiary with a brief description of your relationship. If you're naming an organization, be as specific as possible in naming it.

The laws of every state allow your spouse to receive a portion of your estate, even if you leave your spouse nothing or just a very small portion of your estate in your Will. For more information, please refer to Chapter One of the Personal Law Topics, or consult with an attorney.

Residuary Share

How do you want your residuary beneficiaries to share your residuary estate?

( ) In equal shares
( ) By percentage

Comment: Make a selection and press [Enter] or select <NEXT> for the next question.

Percentage Share

Here are the names of your residuary beneficiaries. Indicate the percentage of your residuary estate you want each of them to receive.

[Example:	*Mary Ellen Doe*	*40*
	Barbara Smith	*30*
	Randall Jones	*20*
	Bonnie Grant	*10]*

Comment: Enter the percentage of your residuary estate that you want each of these beneficiaries to receive. The program will tell you if the amounts you enter don't total 100%. Select <NEXT> to continue.

Predeceased Residuary

If one of your residuary beneficiaries fails to survive you by 30 days, how do you want to dispose of that share of your residuary estate?

( ) Children of Beneficiary then Other Named Residuary Beneficiaries
( ) Give Directly to Other Named Residuary Beneficiaries

Comment: Mark your selection and press [Enter] or select <NEXT> to continue.

A. Give it to the children of the deceased beneficiary, in equal shares. If no children, the other named residuary beneficiary or beneficiaries will take this share.

B. Give it directly to the other named residuary beneficiary or beneficiaries who survive you.

By designating the manner in which your residuary estate will be divided if one of your beneficiaries dies before you do, you'll avoid delay in the probate of your estate, and prevent a portion of your estate from going to the state.

How Many Alternates

How many alternate beneficiaries would you like to specify?

( ) One Alternate
( ) Two or more Alternates

Comment: Your alternate choice will receive this portion of your residuary estate only if your first choice fails to survive you by 30 days.

Multiple Alternates

Enter the name of the person(s) or organization(s) you want to designate as an alternate to receive your residuary beneficiary's share of your residuary estate.

[Example: my son, James Norris]

Comment: Enter the full legal name. If you're naming an organization, be as specific as possible in naming it. If you enter more than one alternate beneficiary, enter each name on a separate line. Press [Enter] to move down a line. Select <NEXT> to move to the next question.

Alternate's Share   **You've named more than one alternate residuary beneficiary. How do you want them to share your residuary estate?**

( ) In Equal Shares
( ) By percentage

Comment: Make a selection and press [Enter] or select <NEXT>.

Alternate's %   **Here is a list of the alternate beneficiaries to your residuary estate. Enter the percentage of your estate you want each of them to receive.**

[Example:	*Mary Ellen Doe*	*40*
	Barbara Smith	*30*
	Randall Jones	*20*
	Bonnie Grant	*10]*

Comment: The program will tell you if the amounts entered don't equal 100 percent. Select <NEXT> to continue.

Predeceased Alternates   **If one of the alternate residuary beneficiaries you've named fails to survive you by 30 days, how do you want to dispose of that share of your residuary estate?**

( ) Children of Alternate Beneficiary then Other Named Alternates
( ) Give Directly to Other Named Alternates

Comment: This will help avoid a delay in the probate of your estate, and prevent a portion of your estate from going to the state.

A. Give it to the deceased alternate beneficiary's children, in equal shares. (If the alternate beneficiary dies without leaving children, this share will go to the other named alternate beneficiaries.)

B. Give it directly to the other named alternate beneficiaries.

By deciding how to divide the portion of your residuary estate that would have gone to an alternate beneficiary who fails to survive you, you avoid delay in the probate of your estate, and prevent a portion of your estate from going to the state.

Single Alternate   **Enter the name of the person or organization you want to designate as an alternate to receive your residuary estate should the residuary beneficiary fail to survive you by 30 days.**

[Example: the Halstead Street Shelter in Hometown, Ohio]

Comment: Please enter the full legal name. If you're naming an organization, be as specific as possible in naming it.

Executor   **Who will be the Executor of your estate?**

This person will be responsible for carrying out the terms of your Will.

[Example: Barbara Cantwell]

Comment: Please use the full legal name of your choice. Do not use social names, nicknames or abbreviations.

The Executor is also sometimes referred to as the "personal representative." This should be someone you trust. The Executor, once approved by the probate court, will have a number of important duties and obligations. Be sure you discuss this with the person you want to name as Executor, and obtain his or her approval.

You should let your Executor know where to find the signed original of your Will, so there will be no delay in the administration of your estate.

Executor Bonded   **Do you want your Executor to be bonded?**

The purpose of bonding your Executor is to protect the value of assets in your estate from the Executor's gross negligence or willful misconduct in handling your estate.

( ) YES
( ) NO

Comment: Keep in mind that the cost of obtaining a bond is an expense of your estate, and in effect reduces the amount you leave your beneficiaries.

Alternate Executor **If this person cannot serve as Executor, who do you want to name as an alternate?**

[Example: Harold Dixon]

Comment: If your first choice as Executor cannot serve for any reason, you should name an alternate choice here.

How to Pay Debts **How do you want to pay unsecured debts and expenses owed by your estate?**

( ) Provided by state law
( ) Out of residuary estate

Comment: You can leave instructions for your Executor regarding the payment of debts you owe when you die.

The two types of debt are unsecured and secured. An unsecured debt would include credit card debts, personal loans, and expenses of your last illness and the probate of your estate.

Option A - specifies that unsecured debts be paid as provided by the laws of your state.

Option B - specifies that unsecured debts be paid out of that part of your estate which is left after all the special gifts and all the expenses have been paid.

If you need advice regarding which option is right for you, you should consult with an attorney for assistance. Your state bar association can provide you with a referral to an attorney who can help you.

Forgive Debts **Do you want to forgive any debts that are owed to you?**

( ) YES
( ) NO

Comment: You cannot forgive a debt if it is jointly owed to you and another person. By answering "YES" to forgive a debt, you are in effect reducing the size of your estate.

Forgiven Debt   **Enter the name of the person or institution whose debt is being forgiven, along with a brief description of the debt.**

[For example, "Martin Long, debt in the amount of $7,000 owed since May 5, 1989."]

Comment: Be as accurate as possible in identifying the debt and the person who owes it. If you're forgiving more than one debt, separate each clause by semi-colons.

You can forgive any debts owed to you personally at the time of your death. But you cannot forgive a debt if it is jointly owed to you and another person (such as your spouse).

Pay Taxes   **How do you want estate or inheritance taxes paid?**

( ) Out of residuary estate
( ) As provided by state law

Comment: In some, but not all states, estates with a total value of less than $600,000 are exempt from federal and state taxes.

We suggest you speak with an attorney who's familiar with estate planning if a) you expect your estate to have a value greater than $600,000, b) you have questions about the threshold for state taxes, or c) you have any questions about the right option for you to use.

Minor Child   **Are any of your child(ren) under the age of 18?**

( ) YES
( ) NO

Comment: Select "YES" or "NO". Press [Enter] or select <NEXT> to move to the next question.

Guardian   **If the other parent of your minor children fails to survive you by 30 days, who will be the Guardian of your minor children?**

Comment: If you fail to name a Guardian, the courts will designate someone to serve in that capacity.

Home Lawyer's Will names the other parent(s) of your minor children as Guardian. If that parent fails to survive you, you should name a person you trust as Guardian.

Be sure to discuss this beforehand with the person you wish to name, so that he or she knows of your wishes and is willing to serve as Guardian.

Alternate Guardian

If this person can't serve as Guardian, who else do you want to name?

Comment: If the person you just named as Guardian fails to survive you, or is unwilling to act as Guardian when the time comes, you can name an alternate Guardian here.

Set up a Trust

Do you want to set up a trust for any of your minor children?

( ) YES
( ) NO

Comment: Select "YES" to set up a trust for your minor children.

Home Lawyer allows you to appoint a person (called a Trustee) to oversee and manage the property you leave to your minor children until they are mature enough to take responsibility for it themselves.

Home Lawyer allows you to create a trust for your minor children. In some states, you have the choice of using Home Lawyer's Support Trust, or using the provisions of your state's Uniform Transfers to Minors Act (UTMA).

The UTMA provides standardized procedures for transferring assets intended for a minor to a Custodian, who manages the assets until the minor reaches the age specified in the law. The major benefits of using the UTMA are that it clearly sets forth the manner for transferring assets as a matter of law, and eliminates any possible confusion about how the transfer should be made.

Type of Trust   **Choose the way you want to establish your minor children's trust.**

( ) Use Home Lawyer's Support Trust
( ) Use State Law

Comment: Please press [F1] for additional comments.

The Uniform Transfers to Minors Act (UTMA) was written and approved in 1983 by the National Conference of Commissioners on Uniform State Laws. The Conference attempts to create model laws and minimize the differences in laws that occur from one state to another.

Basically, the UTMA provides standardized procedures for transferring assets intended for a minor to a Custodian, who manages the assets until the minor reaches the age specified in the law. The major benefits of using the UTMA is that it clearly sets forth the manner for transferring assets as a matter of law, and eliminates any possible confusion about how the transfer should be made.

The ultimate responsibility for adopting a uniform law remains with each state's legislature and not every state has adopted the UTMA. In addition, some states have amended the model UTMA. If you have any questions about the UTMA in your state, we recommend that you contact your county law library, or consult with an attorney experienced in estate planning.

While using your state's Uniform Transfers to Minors Act can simplify the administration of your trust (since banks, lawyers, and courts are probably more familiar with the requirements of the law than they may be with the terms of Home Lawyer's Support Trust), you cannot extend the age at which the trust ends and the minor receives the gift outright.

In Alabama, Alaska, Arizona, Arkansas, Colorado, Florida, Georgia, Hawaii, Idaho, Illinois, Indiana, Iowa, Kansas, Maine, Maryland, Massachusetts, Minnesota, Montana, New Hampshire, New Jersey, New Mexico, North Carolina, North Dakota, Ohio, Oregon, Utah, Virginia, West Virginia, Wisconsin and Wyoming, the trust will end when the minor reaches 21 years of age.

In California, the trust must end when the minor reaches 25 years of age.

In Kentucky, Nevada, Oklahoma, Rhode Island, South Dakota and the District of Columbia, the trust must end when the minor reaches 18 years of age.

If you decide to use Home Lawyer's trust, you can designate an age up to 35 for the age when the trust will terminate for a given child. If you're concerned about a child's maturity or ability to handle property you're leaving, you may want to use Home Lawyer's trust provisions instead.

HL Trust Age   **Here are the names of your children. Press [Tab] and enter the age at which Home Lawyer's trust should expire for each child. Enter an age between 18 and 35.**

Comment: If you do not want to establish a trust for one of your children, highlight the child's name and press [F2] to delete. Select <NEXT> to continue.

The trust will expire when each child reaches the age you designate. For each child, you should choose an age at which you believe he or she will be mature enough to assume full ownership of the property you are leaving.

UTMA Names   **Here are the names of your children. If you do not want to establish a trust for one of them under your state's Uniform Transfers to Minors Act, highlight that child's name and press [F2] to delete.**

Comment: The trust will expire when each child reaches the age designated under state law.

Trustee   **Enter the name of the person or institution you want to serve as Trustee.**

Comment: The person you named as Guardian may also be entered here.

The Trustee will be responsible for managing the property in the trust. You may choose anyone you consider honest and trustworthy, including a friend, family member, or business associate. You may wish to name the same person who will serve as Guardian, so there will be no possibility of disagreement about the use of trust property for the health, education and well-being of your children.

While you can name a bank or trust company as Trustee, it may not be in your best interests to do so. Financial institutions' fees for managing a trust can be substantial, and the trust may be combined and managed with others. For more information, see the Establishing Trusts section in Chapter One of the Personal Law Topics, or consult with an attorney who's familiar with estate planning techniques. If your state has adopted the Uniform Transfers to Minors Act, and you chose that trust option, the Trustee will be referred to as the Custodian.

Alt Trustee   **If your first choice cannot serve as Trustee, enter the name of your alternate choice.**

Comment: The person you named as Guardian may also be entered.

Give Funeral Instructions   **Do you want to leave any instructions about your funeral, burial or cremation in your Last Will and Testament?**

( ) YES
( ) NO

Comment: Select "YES" or "NO".

Funeral Instructions   **Enter any instructions you want to leave regarding your funeral and burial or cremation. Please enter these instructions in a full sentence or sentences.**

Comment: You may enter any special instructions regarding your funeral and the disposition of your remains here.

You should remember that some time may elapse between your death and the reading of your Will. Be sure to convey your wishes about this matter to someone who will be able to see that they are honored, in addition to entering them here.

Disinherit   **Do you want to disinherit anyone who contests your Will?**

( ) YES
( ) NO

Comment: You can choose to disinherit anyone who challenges any of your Will's provisions.

For example, if one of your children is unhappy with the property you leave him or her, and decides to contest your Will, this provision prevents that child from receiving any of your property, even that which you might have left to him or her. A will contest can be lengthy and expensive, and cause great delay in the probate of your estate.

Sample Document[1]

LAST WILL AND TESTAMENT
OF
Karen S. Jones

I, Karen S. Jones, of Cleveland, Ohio, being of sound mind and under no restraint, hereby publish and declare this instrument to be my Last Will and Testament, revoking all previous Wills and Codicils I have made. My social security number is 111-22-3333.

I am not married to any person. I have no children.

ITEM I

I hereby give my friend, Martha J. Stewart, my antique diamond and ruby ring. In the event Martha J. Stewart shall fail to survive me, this gift shall go instead to my niece, Robin J. Jones. If neither beneficiary named in this paragraph survives me, this gift becomes part of my residuary estate.

ITEM II

I give the entire residue of my estate, whether real, personal or mixed, to my brother, Jeff J. Jones, and my sister, Brenda K. Jones, in equal shares, share and share alike. If any residuary beneficiary named herein fails to survive me, then that beneficiary's share shall be divided among the living children of said beneficiary, in equal shares, share and share alike. If any residuary beneficiary named herein fails to survive me, and if said beneficiary leaves no living children, then that beneficiary's share of my residuary estate shall be divided among the beneficiaries who did survive me, in equal shares, share and share alike.

ITEM III

I nominate and appoint Barbara Cantwell as Executor of this, my Last Will and Testament. My Executor shall be required to post bond. If the above-named Executor is unable or unwilling to serve, or otherwise fails to complete the administration of my estate, I nominate and appoint Robert Anderson instead. Said Executor shall be required to post bond.

ITEM IV

I direct my Executor to pay all of my legally enforceable debts, the expenses of my funeral and burial or cremation, and the expenses of the administration of my estate in the manner prescribed by state law.

---

[1] The sample document has been prepared and formatted for illustration purposes only. The actual document will print using the standard type style of your printer and the number of lines per page may differ.

ITEM V

In addition to the powers conferred on my Executor by law, I authorize my Executor to do all acts which my Executor deems necessary or appropriate in order to achieve the purposes of this, my Last Will and Testament, including the power to sell or dispose of property and distribute the proceeds of such sale or disposal as part of my estate; to retain property without liability for any depreciation or loss which may result; to settle, compromise, or abandon any claim either for or against my estate; to vote stock or exercise any of the rights of ownership of any stocks or bonds which form a part of this estate; to continue or participate in the operations of any business which forms a part of this estate, all as fully as I could do if living.

ITEM VI

I authorize my Executor to utilize the services of an attorney, accountant and any other professional as may be necessary or desirable in the administration of this, my Last Will and Testament. The expenses incurred by my Executor using such professional services shall be an expense to my estate and shall be paid by my estate.

ITEM VII

I direct my Executor to pay out of the assets of my residuary estate, all inheritance, transfer, estate and similar taxes (including interest and penalties) on any property or interest in property included in my estate for the purpose of computing taxes. My Executor shall not require any beneficiary under this Will to reimburse my estate for taxes paid on property passing under the terms of this Will.

ITEM VIII

My Executor named herein shall be entitled to reasonable compensation commensurate with the services actually performed and to reimbursement for expenses properly incurred.

ITEM IX

It is not my intention to make provision in this, my Last Will and Testament, for any relative or any other person not expressly provided for herein, except for children born to or legally adopted by me after the date of this instrument, and if any such person has not been expressly mentioned herein, he or she has been omitted by me intentionally and with full knowledge of his or her relationship and existence, and not by any oversight or neglect.

ITEM X

If, subsequent to the execution of this, my Last Will and Testament, there shall be any child or children born to or legally adopted by me, such child or children shall share in the benefits of my estate to the same extent as he or she would have shared had I died without a Will, and the provisions of this Will shall be modified to the extent necessary to see that this is done.

ITEM XI

Where appropriate to the context, pronouns or other terms expressed in one number or gender shall be deemed to include the other number or gender, as the case may be.

ITEM XII

Any person or organization named or referred to herein shall be deemed to have survived me only if such person or organization shall in fact survive me for a period of at least thirty (30) days. Any person or organization named or referred to herein who shall not survive me for a period of at least thirty (30) days shall be deemed to have died before I do.

IN WITNESS WHEREOF, I have signed my name, declaring and publishing this instrument as my Last Will and Testament, in the presence of the undersigned Witnesses on this _____ day of _____, 19__.

_____
Karen S. Jones

ATTESTATION

We hereby certify that this Last Will and Testament was signed, declared and published by Karen S. Jones as her Last Will and Testament on this day, in our presence and in the presence of each other, and we sign our names below as Witnesses in her presence, at her request and in the presence of each other on this _____ day of _____, 19___.

Resides at

_____   _____
Witness 1 Signature   Street Address

_____   _____
Witness 1 Name (Printed)   City, State, Zip

Resides at

_____   _____
Witness 2 Signature   Street Address

Resides at

_____   _____
Witness 2 Name (Printed)   City, State, Zip

Resides at

_____   _____
Witness 3 Signature   Street Address

Resides at

_____   _____
Witness 3 Name (Printed)   City, State, Zip

AFFIDAVIT

We, _____, _____,
_____, and _____, the Testator and
Witnesses, having first been duly sworn, do solemnly swear that in our presence and in the
presence of each other, Karen S. Jones signed, declared and published the foregoing
instrument on _____, 19____, as her Last Will and Testament,
and asked each of us to serve as Witnesses. Each of the Witnesses signed this Last Will
and Testament as Witnesses, in the presence of Karen S. Jones and in the presence of each
other. At the time of signing this Last Will and Testament, Karen S. Jones appeared to us
to be of sound mind, free from duress, fraud or undue influence. Each of us who signed
the foregoing instrument as a Witness is twenty-one (21) years of age or older and fully
competent to serve as a Witness.

_____ _____
Date   Karen S. Jones, Testator

_____ _____
Date   Witness 1

_____ _____
Date   Witness 2

_____ _____
Date   Witness 3

Subscribed and sworn to before me by _____,
_____, _____, and
_____, each of whom is known to me personally, this _____
day of _____, 19____.

My Commission Expires:

_____ _____
                                               NOTARY PUBLIC

(SEAL)

SOME SUGGESTIONS
ABOUT YOUR WILL

Before your Last Will and Testament becomes valid, it must be properly executed. Although state laws vary, these steps should enable you to make your Last Will and Testament valid in your state (except Louisiana).

1.   You will need three witnesses. You should sign your Will in front of the three of them at the same time. As you sign it, tell them that this document is your Last Will and Testament and that you are asking them to sign it as witnesses. (You may also want to initial each page to prevent anyone from making alterations to your Will. If you do, initial it at the bottom of each page, and have your Witnesses put their initials next to yours.) You do not have to reveal the contents of your Will to your Witnesses.

2.   Have the Witnesses sign on the appropriate lines. You must watch each Witness sign, and each of them must watch the others sign.

3.   In most states, the Affidavit that printed with your Will allows your Executor to begin the probate of your estate without having to call your Witnesses to court to prove that your Will is really your Will. (This is called "proving" the Will; the affidavit is called a "self-proving" affidavit.)

To make your Will self-proving, you should read and sign the affidavit on the line indicated. Your Witnesses should read the affidavit and sign it in your presence, in the presence of each other, and in the presence of a notary public.

While certain states do not recognize self-proving affidavits, having one anyway will not affect your Will's validity. Neither will not having one in states that honor them. The choice is yours.

Your Witnesses should be at least 21 years old, and they should not include anyone who will receive any of your property under your Will.

DO NOT sign any copies of your Will, or make copies of your signed Will. Sign only the original, using the procedure outlined above.

DO NOT make any changes, alterations or additions to your Will once it is printed. If you need to make a change, go back to the program and print a new document. Be sure to destroy the incorrect Will immediately, so there is no confusion later about which version is the correct one.

Keep the executed original of your Will in a safe place. A fireproof file box or home safe is usually better than a bank safety deposit box, since some states seal the box on your death.

This could delay the probate of your estate. Wherever you keep your executed Will, be sure to tell someone you trust (for example, your Executor) where it can be found in the event of your death. Attaching a list of your assets (insurance policy numbers, bank account information, etc.) will help your Executor carry out your wishes with a minimum of delay.

Living Will

Document Summary

A Living Will is a directive to physicians, instructing them of your desire to have life-prolonging measures withheld or withdrawn in the event of a terminal illness.

It is signed, dated, and witnessed with many of the same formalities as a Last Will and Testament.

Currently, 42 states and the District of Columbia have enacted statutes setting out the requirements for creating a valid Living Will. In those states that have yet to enact Living Will statutes, a Living Will can still be a useful way to inform your doctor and other health care professionals of your desires.

In 1990, the United States Supreme Court ruled that a state may require clear and convincing evidence of your wishes before permitting the withdrawal of life-prolonging medical procedures. A Living Will can provide such clear and convincing evidence.

A Living Will which, in advance, describes your wish to have life-prolonging medical procedures withheld or withdrawn can also help to relieve your family of the burden of making an uninformed decision about your treatment if you become unable to participate in making decisions about your own medical care.

A Living Will can permit you to die with dignity, and may spare you years of a comatose existence. Medical technology has achieved a great deal in prolonging lives. But in many cases, although life is prolonged, there is no way for the person to return to a meaningful or productive life. If you would prefer not to live a life that can be prolonged but not improved, a Living Will lets you inform your physician of this fact.

Finally, a Living Will serves as a means of protection for doctors, hospitals and family members who must ultimately decide when to withdraw or withhold medical treatment. A Living Will protects them from claims by the state or by other family members that they acted in disregard of your preference for medical treatment.

Home Lawyer's Living Will is designed to meet the requirements of the law in the state where you live. If you move from one state to another, we suggest that you create a new Living Will that meets the legal requirements of your new home state.

In most states, any adult over the age of 18 may make a Living Will. New Mexico, Oklahoma, and Vermont require the person making a Living Will (called the declarant) to be at least 21 years of age. Witnesses to your Living Will should be at least 18 years of age, except in New Mexico, Oklahoma, and Vermont, where the witnesses should be at least 21 years old.

Once you have answered Home Lawyer's questions, you'll be ready to print your Living Will. It is very important that you read this document carefully. The documents for some states will require you to provide certain other information regarding your wishes about life-prolonging medical treatment. Follow the instructions on your Living Will for providing this information.

You may revoke your Living Will at any time. Home Lawyer contains a document that allows you to revoke your Living Will.

If you decide to revoke your Living Will, you should attach a copy of your original Living Will to the revocation. You should also be sure to provide a copy of the revocation to anyone who received a copy of your Living Will.

For more information about Living Wills, you can consult with an attorney familiar with the laws in your state, or contact your county law library. You may also wish to write to:

CONCERN FOR THE DYING/
SOCIETY FOR THE RIGHT TO DIE
250 West 57th Street
New York, NY 10107

to obtain more information about Living Will laws.

Questions and Comments

Note: The following describes every question for a Living Will. However, during the Question and Answer session, the program will display only those questions relevant to the laws of your state.

Legal Name

Please enter your full legal name.

[Example: Jonathan A. Doe]

Comment: Do not use any nicknames or abbreviations. The name must be your legal name, not your social name.

For example, the proper way to name John Smith's wife is Barbara S. Smith; it is not correct to use Mrs. John Smith.

User State

This is the state where you live.

Comment: If this is incorrect, press [Esc] to exit. Re-select Living Will and make sure you correctly identify your state of residence from the list box.

Male/Female

Choose your gender.

( ) Male
( ) Female

Comment: This choice controls gender replacement within the document.

City

Enter the name of the city where you live.

[Example: Chicago]

Comment: Enter the name of the city, town, or village you live in, but don't use the name of a real estate subdivision. For example, if you live in the Blair Estate subdivision of Shaker, use Shaker.

User Address

Enter your street address.

[Example: 1270 Anystreet, Suite 135]

Comment: When the mailing address is more than one line, use commas to separate each part.

County Name   **In what county do you live?**

[Example: Mason]

Comment: In Louisiana, enter your Parish here. In Alaska, enter your Judicial District here.

Proxy   **Do you want to name a person who will serve as your health care proxy?**

Your health care proxy is the person who will ultimately decide whether to withhold or withdraw life-prolonging measures.

( ) YES
( ) NO

Comment: You may name a person who will bear the responsibility for making the final decision to withdraw or withhold medical treatment. If you do not name a proxy, this decision will usually be left to your closest relative.

Proxy Name   **Enter the name of the person you want to serve as your health care proxy.**

Note: This can be any person you trust, such as a family member or close personal friend.

Comment: You should discuss your wishes about such treatment in advance with the person you select, and obtain his or her consent to serve in this capacity.

Proxy Address   **Enter the street address of your health care proxy.**

[Example: 1313 Mockingbird Lane, Apt 206]

Comment: This is your health care proxy's home address.

Proxy CSZ   **Enter the city, state, and zip code of your health care proxy.**

[Example: Minneapolis, MN 55330]

Comment: Use the two letter abbreviation for your state.

Proxy Phone	**Enter your health care proxy's telephone number.**

[Example: (612) 241-1234]

Comment: Press [Enter] or select <NEXT> to continue.

Proxy Relation	**Enter a brief description of your relationship with the health care proxy named above.**

[Example: My Friend]

Comment: One or two words will do here. For example, "My Mother."

Food and Water	**Enter your choice regarding the provision of food or water by gastric tube or intravenous feeding.**

( ) I do want food or water provided
( ) I do not want food or water provided

Comment: State law allows you to direct your physician as to whether or not to provide you with food ("nutrition") or water ("hydration") when you become unable to eat or drink.

SSN User	**Please enter your Social Security Number here.**

Comment: Your Social Security Number helps to further identify you as the declarant, and is required by Mississippi law.

Next of Kin	**Enter the name of your next of kin.**

Note: Your next of kin is your spouse, if you are married.

Comment: If you are not married, your next of kin is your nearest living blood relative. Mississippi law requires you to provide this information.

Kin Address	**Enter the street address of your next of kin.**

[Example: 1313 Mockingbird Lane, Apt. 206]

Comment: This is your next of kin's current home address.

Kin CSZ   **Enter the city, state, and zip code of your next of kin.**

[Example: Beachwood, OH 44122]

Comment: Use the two letter abbreviation for the state.

Physician   **Enter your physician's name here.**

Comment: In Vermont, your physician is required by state law to make your Living Will a part of your medical records.

Sample Document[1]

LIVING WILL DECLARATION

To My Family, Physician and Medical Facility:

I, Janet P. Williams, being of sound mind, voluntarily make known my desire that my dying not be artificially prolonged under the circumstances:

If I should have an injury, disease or illness regarded by my physician as incurable and terminal, and if my physician determines that the application of life-sustaining procedures would serve only to prolong artificially the dying process, I direct that such procedures be withheld or withdrawn and that I be permitted to die. I want treatment limited to those measures that will provide me with maximum comfort and freedom from pain. Should I become unable to participate in decisions with respect to my medical treatment, it is my intention that these directions be honored by my family and physicians as a final expression of my legal right to refuse medical treatment, and I accept the consequences of this refusal.

Date: _____   Signed: _____
                               Janet P. Williams

_____   _____
Witness   Witness

---

[1] The sample document has been prepared and formatted for illustration purposes only. The actual document will print using the standard type style of your printer and the number of lines per page may differ.

DESIGNATION CLAUSE

Should I become comatose, incompetent or otherwise mentally or physically incapable of communication, I authorize Alice B. Thomas to make treatment decisions on my behalf in accordance with my Living Will Declaration. I have discussed my wishes concerning medical care with this person and I trust Alice B. Thomas's judgment on my behalf.

Date: _____   Signed: _____
                                      Janet P. Williams

Witness _____   Witness _____

ACKNOWLEDGEMENT

State of Ohio   )
) ss.
County of Franklin   )

    On this _____ day of _____, 19__, before me, the undersigned Notary Public, personally appeared Janet P. Williams, known to me or satisfactorily proven to be the person whose name is subscribed to the above Living Will Declaration, and acknowledged that she executed the same for the purpose expressed therein. Further, said person appeared to be of sound mind and under no duress, fraud or undue influence.

                              _____
                              Notary Public

                              My Commission Expires: _____

Revocation of Living Will

Document Summary

This document allows you to create a written revocation of a Living Will. A written revocation is the best way to notify your physicians and other health care professionals of your desire to revoke a Living Will which you have previously made.

State laws allow you to revoke your Living Will at any time. While an oral revocation is considered valid, using a written revocation will ensure that there is no confusion about your wishes to receive life-prolonging medical procedures in the event of a terminal illness.

You should provide a copy of this Revocation of Living Will to anyone who received a copy of your Living Will. If your Living Will was made part of your medical records by your doctor or at a hospital or other health care facility, this Revocation should be included in those records as well.

Questions and Comments

Note: The following describes _every_ question for the Revocation of Living Will. However, during the Question and Answer session, the program will display only those questions relevant to the laws of your state.

Revoke Name   **Enter your name as it appears on your Living Will.**

[Example: John Doe]

Comment: Enter your full legal name as it appears on your Living Will. Do not use any abbreviations or nicknames.

Current State   **Enter the name of the state in which you currently reside.**

Comment: Use the two-letter abbreviation for the state.

Which State	**Did you create your Living Will in the District of Columbia, Mississippi or another state?** *( ) Other State* *( ) District of Columbia* *( ) Mississippi* **Comment:** Make the desired selection and press [Enter] or select <NEXT> to continue.
State for Will	**Enter the name of the state in which you lived at the time you made the Living Will.** **Comment:** Use the two-letter abbreviation for the state.
SSN	**Please enter your Social Security Number here.** **Comment:** Your Social Security Number helps to further identify you as the declarant, and is required by Mississippi law.
User Address	**Enter your street address.** *[Example: 1270 Anystreet, Suite 135]* **Comment:** When the mailing address is more than one line, use commas to separate each part.
User CSZ	**Enter your city, state and zip code.** *[Example: Jacksonville, MS 98139]* **Comment:** Use the name of the community as named by the United States Post Office. Do not use the name of a real estate subdivision unless it is used as a Post Office address. Enter the city, state, zip code. Use the two-letter state abbreviation, and use at least the five digit zip code. The state abbreviations are listed under the Help Topics.

Will Date   **Enter the date on which you and your witnesses executed your Living Will.**

[Example: 01/01/1992]

Comment: This is the date on which you signed your original Living Will in the presence of your witnesses.

Sample Document[1]

REVOCATION OF LIVING WILL

On this _____ day of _____, 19__, I, John Q. Public,

being of sound mind and under no duress, willfully and voluntarily revoke the Living Will

Declaration made by me on October 1st, 1991, while a resident of Ohio, a copy of which is

attached to this Revocation.

By this Revocation, I hereby declare that the aforementioned Living Will

Declaration is null and void from this date forward.

_____

John Q. Public

---

[1] The sample document has been prepared and formatted for illustration purposes only. The actual document will print using the standard type style of your printer and the number of lines per page may differ.

ATTESTATION

I hereby witness this Revocation and attest that John Q. Public is personally known to me, and I believe John Q. Public to be of sound mind. I saw John Q. Public, the maker of this Revocation, sign it in my presence, freely and voluntarily, and I signed the Revocation as a Witness in the presence of the maker. I did not sign the maker's signature above for or at the maker's direction.

As of this date, I am not entitled to any portion of the estate of John Q. Public according to the laws of intestate succession, or, to the best of my knowledge and belief, under any Will of the maker, or any other instrument taking effect upon the death of the maker. I am not related to the maker by blood or marriage. I am not John Q. Public's attending physician, nor an employee of or patient in a health care facility in which the maker of this Revocation is a patient. I am not directly financially responsible for the medical care of the maker. I am of sufficient legal age to serve as a Witness to this Revocation under the laws of Ohio.

_____   _____
Witness   Witness

_____   _____
Address   Address

_____   _____
City, State and Zip   City, State and Zip

NOTARY'S STATEMENT

State of Ohio   )
) ss.
County of _____   )

    I, _____, a notary public in and for the state and county named above, hereby certify that on the _____ day of _____, 19__, personally appeared John Q. Public, the maker of this Revocation, and _____ and _____, Witnesses, and that, having first been duly sworn, they signed the above instrument in my presence and in the presence of each other, freely and voluntarily, and for the purposes described therein.

_____
Notary Public

My Commission Expires:_____

General Power of Attorney

Document Summary

Home Lawyer's General Power of Attorney allows one person (the Principal) to give very broad powers to another person (the Attorney-in-fact) to act on the Principal's behalf. With a General Power of Attorney, you can give another person the power to do anything on your behalf that you could do yourself - for example, sell and buy real estate or other property, open bank accounts or stock brokerage accounts, operate your business, use your credit, and so on.

Generally, you can name anyone you know and trust to be your Attorney-in-fact, provided that he or she is of sound mind and legal age. Your spouse, an accountant, a real estate broker, a friend or relative, even a lawyer can serve as your Attorney-in-fact.

Note: State laws may prohibit your spouse from serving as your Attorney-in-fact for the purpose of conveying real estate. If you want your Attorney-in-fact to sell, exchange, or otherwise transfer title to real estate you own, we strongly recommend that you designate someone other than your spouse as your Attorney-in-fact.

If you want your Attorney-in-fact to be able to continue to act as your agent in the event you become mentally incapacitated, you should select the Durable Power of Attorney option. Otherwise, your Attorney-in-fact's authorization to act on your behalf will expire when you become mentally incapacitated.

When should you use a General Power of Attorney? When you'll be out of the country for an extended period of time and need someone to pay your bills and collect your income; or whenever you need someone to act on your behalf in a variety of ways.

Even though a Power of Attorney can remain in effect almost indefinitely (unless you name an expiration date, only the death of the Principal or a Revocation will terminate a Durable Power of Attorney), some experts suggest you renew the Power of Attorney annually, so there's no doubt that it continues in effect.

In many states, you will need to record the Power of Attorney in a government office. You should record any Power of Attorney that deals with real property in the office where deeds are recorded. Your state may have other recording requirements as well. You can contact your county law librarian or an attorney for the specific requirements in your state.

If you only want your Attorney-in-fact to act in a limited way on your behalf, or if you want your Attorney-in-fact to authorize medical treatment for your minor children, do not use the General Power of Attorney. Use Home Lawyer's Medical/Special Power of Attorney instead.

Questions and Comments

Note: The following describes <u>every</u> question for the General Power of Attorney. However, during the Question and Answer session, the program will display only those questions relevant to your personal situation.

Durable POA

Do you want to create a Durable Power of Attorney?

( ) YES
( ) NO

Comment: A Durable Power of Attorney will remain in effect even if you become disabled or incapacitated. Otherwise, it will expire upon your disability, or on a date you select.

Select "YES" if you want this Power of Attorney to be durable. This means the Power of Attorney will continue to be effective even if you suffer a disabling injury or are otherwise unable to care for yourself.

Select "NO" if you want this Power of Attorney to expire should you become disabled or incapacitated.

This document will give the person you name the power to act in your place, to transact business and to manage your affairs in your name. While the Power of Attorney is in effect, you will be bound by the actions of your Attorney-in-fact as if they were your own.

The Power of Attorney will remain in effect from the time it starts until you revoke it (see Revocation of Power of Attorney).

Legal Name

Please enter your full legal name.

[Example: Jonathan A. Doe]

Comment: Do not use any nicknames or abbreviations. The name must be the legal name, not the social name.

Male/Female   **Choose your gender.**

( ) Male
( ) Female

Comment: This choice controls gender replacement within the document.

County Name   **In what county do you live?**

[Example: Mason]

Comment: In Louisiana, enter your Parish here. In Alaska, enter your Judicial District here.

County Type   **Select the appropriate designation.**

[Example: County]

Note: In Louisiana select Parish, in Alaska select Judicial District, and for most other states select County.

( ) County
( ) Parish
( ) Judicial District
( ) Other

Comment: Select County, Parish or Judicial District. Select Other if none of these apply.

Other Territory   **Please enter the designation for your location.**

Comment: Be sure to capitalize the first letter.

State   **Enter the state where you live.**

[Example: IL]

Comment: Use the two-letter abbreviation for your state.

Atty In Fact	**Enter the full legal name of the person who will be your Attorney-in-fact.**

[Example: James S. Alexander]

Comment: Your Attorney-in-fact is the person who will act on your behalf as authorized by this Power of Attorney.

This should be a person you trust, as you are delegating important responsibilities, and you will be bound by your Attorney-in-fact's actions as if they were your own.

Real Estate	**Do you presently own real estate?**

( ) YES
( ) NO

Comment: Some states require a description of the real estate you own for the Power of Attorney to be valid.

If you do not presently own, but subsequently acquire, real estate, you will want to prepare a new Power of Attorney to include a description of the real estate you acquire.

Real County Name	**Enter the county in which the real estate you own is located.**

[Example: Mason]

Note: In Louisiana, enter the Parish. In Alaska, enter the Judicial District.

Comment: This Power of Attorney enables your Attorney-in-fact to sell, mortgage, lease and/or do anything with regard to your real estate that you could do yourself.

Real County Type	**Select the appropriate designation for your real estate.**

In Louisiana select Parish, in Alaska select Judicial District, and for most other states select County.

( ) County
( ) Parish
( ) Judicial District
( ) Other

Comment: Select County, Parish or Judicial District. Select Other if none of these apply.

Real Territory   **Please enter the designation for your real estate.**

Comment: Be sure to capitalize the first letter.

Real State   **Enter the state in which the real estate you own is located.**

[Example: OH]

Comment: This General Power of Attorney enables your Attorney-in-fact to sell, mortgage, lease and/or do anything with regard to your real estate that you could do yourself.

Real Describe   **Enter the legal description of the real estate covered by this Power of Attorney.**

Note: Do not follow the description with a period (.)

Comment: You must enter the legal description exactly as it appears in your deed. An inaccurate entry could prevent your Attorney-in-fact from acting on your behalf.

Execute Date   **Enter the date of execution of this Power of Attorney.**

[Example: 09/28/91]

Comment: This is the date when you will sign the Power of Attorney and have it witnessed and notarized. It may be a date in the future and not today's date.

If you own real estate, this Power of Attorney must also be filed in the office where deeds are recorded in the county where the real estate is located. If you chose to create a Durable Power of Attorney, your state may also require this Durable Power of Attorney to be filed with another public office.

Expire?   **Do you want to set a specific termination date for this Power of Attorney?**

( ) YES
( ) NO

Comment: Select YES if you want to designate a specific termination date. Otherwise select NO.

If you select a specific termination date, your Power of Attorney will expire upon the earlier of that date or your disability or incapacity. If you chose to create a Durable Power of Attorney, it will expire upon the date you select regardless of your prior disability or incapacity.

Expire Date   **Enter the date when you want this Power of Attorney to expire.**

[Example: 09/28/1992]

Comment: Unless Durable, your Power of Attorney will expire either on this date, or upon your disability or incapacity, whichever comes first. If Durable, it will expire on this date.

Sample Document[1]

DURABLE POWER OF ATTORNEY

NOTICE: THIS POWER OF ATTORNEY IS A LEGAL DOCUMENT, AND PROVIDES THE ATTORNEY-IN-FACT WITH BROAD POWERS OVER THE PRINCIPAL'S PROPERTY UNLESS LIMITED BY THE TERMS OF THE POWER OF ATTORNEY ITSELF. THE POWERS GIVEN TO THE ATTORNEY-IN-FACT MAY EXIST FOR AN UNLIMITED PERIOD OF TIME UNLESS LIMITED BY THE TERMS OF THE POWER OF ATTORNEY ITSELF. THE PRINCIPAL MAY REVOKE OR TERMINATE THIS POWER OF ATTORNEY AT ANY TIME. IF YOU NEED ADDITIONAL ADVICE ABOUT THIS POWER OF ATTORNEY, CONSULT WITH A LAWYER BEFORE SIGNING IT.

I, James B. Monroe, of the County of Mason, State of Illinois, hereby appoint Theresa K. Moore as my Attorney-in-fact, giving my Attorney-in-fact full power and authority to do anything I would be entitled to do myself, including but not limited to the following:

To lease, sell, exchange, convey and mortgage any of my real estate or parts of my real estate for whatever consideration and under whatever terms my Attorney-in-fact deems appropriate and proper.

To foreclose mortgages and to take title to real property in my name as my Attorney-in-fact deems appropriate and proper.

To execute, acknowledge and deliver deeds of real estate, deeds of trust, mortgages, releases and any and all other instruments relating to my real estate which my Attorney-in-fact deems appropriate and proper.

To sell any of my real, personal or other property on any terms, and to use the proceeds of such sale in any manner whatsoever.

To buy any real, personal, or other property on my behalf and on any terms.

To use, maintain, manage and insure my property in any manner.

To invest any of my money or other real or personal or other property in any manner.

To borrow money, use credit cards and accounts, mortgage, pledge or otherwise encumber any of my property.

---

[1] The sample document has been prepared and formatted for illustration purposes only. The actual document will print using the standard type style of your printer and the number of lines per page may differ.

To do anything I could do myself with regard to retirement and pension benefits or other benefits of employment, and Social Security benefits. I designate my Attorney-in-fact as representative Payee for my Social Security benefits.

To do anything I could do myself with regard to bank accounts, accounts at savings and loan institutions, credit unions and any other institution, including opening, modifying and closing such accounts and signing and endorsing checks or drafts of all kinds.

To do anything I could do myself with regard to safe deposit boxes, including opening and closing such boxes.

To do anything I could do myself with regard to life insurance policies on myself or anyone else in whom I may have an insurable interest.

To do anything I could do myself with regard to trusts created by me or which exist for my benefit.

To do anything I could do myself with regard to any tax matters or tax returns, including the power to sign any power of attorney form required by the Internal Revenue Service or any other federal, state or local tax authority.

To do anything I could do myself with regard to any legal suit, action or claim.

To do anything I could do myself with regard to the operation of any business or any interest in any business I may have.

To make gifts of my money or property to any person, or to lend my money or other property to any person on any terms whatsoever.

In addition to the powers enumerated above, I give my Attorney-in-fact full power and authority to perform whatever acts are necessary to be done in the premises, and I hereby ratify and confirm any and every act my Attorney-in-fact may lawfully do, acknowledging such acts as my own.

A photocopy of this instrument shall be deemed an original for all purposes.

The real estate referred to in this Power of Attorney is located in King County, California, and is legally described as:

P.P. #271-02-920 Situated in northwest corner of Monroe Orchards also known as 2100 Cedar Road situated in the Village of Roscoe.

This Power of Attorney shall terminate on January 1st, 1993. This Power of Attorney shall not be affected by my disability or incapacity. It is my intent that this instrument be construed as a Durable Power of Attorney.

AN EXECUTED COPY OF THIS POWER OF ATTORNEY SHALL BE FILED IN THE COUNTY WHERE THE REAL ESTATE DESCRIBED HEREIN IS LOCATED, IN THE OFFICE WHERE DEEDS ARE RECORDED. IF STATE LAW REQUIRES THAT A POWER OF ATTORNEY BE FILED IN ANY PUBLIC OFFICE IN ORDER TO BE A LEGALLY ACCEPTED DURABLE POWER OF ATTORNEY, I DIRECT MY ATTORNEY-IN-FACT TO FILE AN EXECUTED COPY OF THIS INSTRUMENT IN SUCH PUBLIC OFFICE.

If any part of this Power of Attorney is held to be invalid under any law, the remainder of this instrument shall not be affected by such invalidity.

IN WITNESS WHEREOF, I have executed this Power of Attorney on October 1st, 1991.

James B. Monroe
Principal

ATTESTATION

We hereby certify that on October 1st, 1991, we witnessed James B. Monroe sign and execute this instrument, declaring and publishing it as his Power of Attorney, in our presence and the presence of each other. We believe James B. Monroe to be of sound mind, under no compulsion or duress, and we sign our names below as Witnesses in his presence, at his request and in the presence of each other on October 1st, 1991.

Resides at

_____   _____
Witness 1 Signature   Street Address

_____   _____
Witness 1 Name (Printed)   City, State, Zip

Resides at

_____   _____
Witness 2 Signature   Street Address

_____   _____
Witness 2 Name (Printed)   City, State, Zip

State of Illinois   )
) ss.
County of Mason   )

On this _____ day of _____, 19___, before me, the undersigned, a Notary Public in and for the State and County named above, personally appeared James B. Monroe, who is known to me personally as the principal described in and who executed the above Power of Attorney, and, after first being sworn, declared this instrument as his free act and deed, and signed it in my presence.

Subscribed and sworn to before me this _____ day of _____, 19___.

My Commission Expires:
_____   _____
                                        NOTARY PUBLIC

(SEAL)

Medical/ Special Power of Attorney

Document Summary

This document allows you (the Principal) to give another (the Attorney-in-fact) specific limited powers regarding your personal affairs and property. It may be used to authorize medical care and treatment for your minor children; to authorize the sale or transfer of real estate on your behalf; or to provide for the sale of items of your personal property.

Generally, you can name anyone you know and trust to be your Attorney-in-fact, provided that he or she is of sound mind and legal age. Your spouse, an accountant, a real estate broker, a friend or relative, even a lawyer can serve as your Attorney-in-fact.

Note: State laws may prohibit your spouse from serving as your Attorney-in-fact for the purpose of conveying real estate. If you want your Attorney-in-fact to sell, exchange, or otherwise transfer title to real estate your own, we strongly recommend that you designate someone other than your spouse as your Attorney-in-fact.

The Medical Power of Attorney can be a real lifesaver. Parents who leave their children in the care of others when they are unable to be reached (on vacation or out of town on business) should have a Medical Power of Attorney prepared before each trip.

A client, whose nephew was in his care while the parents were away, was faced with a scary example of how important this document can be. His toddler nephew was reaching for a pair of scissors on a shelf. The scissors fell and lodged deep in the child's leg. Our client rushed the child to the nearby emergency room. The nurse asked for the child's name and our client's name. When the nurse realized that the adult bringing in the child was not the parent, the nurse requested a "Medical Power of Attorney". "What's that?" our client replied. He was then informed that the hospital could not provide medical attention without the consent of the child's guardian (the parent) or written authority contained in a Medical Power of Attorney.

The lesson learned here is that no one but the parent can authorize medical (even emergency) treatment for your child. The document you prepare using Home Lawyer will protect your children in the event of this kind of emergency.

If you want your Attorney-in-fact to sell, convey, or buy real estate, be sure to enter an accurate description of the real estate. You can copy this information from the deed on the property. Failure to enter an accurate description may prevent your Attorney-in-fact from acting on your behalf, or cause unnecessary delay.

Home Lawyer's Medical/Special Power of Attorney automatically expires three months after the date of its execution unless you specify an earlier expiration date.

You will need to complete and execute a new Power of Attorney if you want the Attorney-in-fact to continue to act on your behalf. If you want your Attorney-in-fact to continue to act on your behalf in the event you become mentally incapacitated before the three-month period expires, you should select the Durable Power of Attorney option.

You should record any Power of Attorney that deals with real property in the office where deeds are recorded. Your state may have other recording requirements as well. You can contact your county law librarian or an attorney for the specific requirements in your state.

If you want to give your Attorney-in-fact broad powers to act on your behalf, you should use Home Lawyer's General Power of Attorney.

Questions and Comments

Note: The following describes every question for the Medical/Special Power of Attorney. However, during the Question and Answer session, the program will display only those questions relevant to your personal situation.

Durable POA

Do you want to create a Durable Power of Attorney?

( ) YES
( ) NO

Comment: A Durable Power of Attorney will remain in effect even if you become disabled or incapacitated. Otherwise, it will expire upon your disability, or on a date you select.

Select "YES" if you want this Power of Attorney to be durable. This means the Power of Attorney will continue to be effective even if you suffer a disabling injury or are otherwise unable to care for yourself.

Select "NO" if you want this Power of Attorney to expire should you become disabled or incapacitated.

This document will give the person you name the power to act in your place, to transact business and to manage your affairs in your name. While the Power of Attorney is in effect, you will be bound by the actions of your Attorney-in-fact as if they were your own.

The Power of Attorney will remain in effect from the time it starts until you revoke it. (See *Revocation of Power of Attorney*.)

Legal Name

Please enter your full legal name.

[Example: Jonathan A. Doe]

Comment: Do not use any nicknames or abbreviations. The name must be the legal name, not the social name.

Male/Female **Choose your gender.**

( ) Male
( ) Female

Comment: This choice controls gender replacement within the document.

County Name **In what county do you live?**

[Example: Mason]

Comment: In Louisiana, enter your Parish here. In Alaska, enter your Judicial District here.

County Type **Select the appropriate designation.**

[Example: County]

Note: In Louisiana select Parish, in Alaska select Judicial District, and for most other states select County.

( ) County
( ) Parish
( ) Judicial District
( ) Other

Comment: Select County, Parish or Judicial District. Select Other if none of these apply.

Other Territory **Please enter the designation for your location.**

Comment: Be sure to capitalize the first letter.

State **Enter the state where you live.**

[Example: IL]

Comment: Use the two-letter abbreviation for your state.

Atty-In-Fact   **Enter the full legal name of the person who will be your Attorney-in-fact.**

[Example: James S. Alexander]

Comment: Your Attorney-in-fact is the person who will act on your behalf as authorized by this Power of Attorney.

This should be a person you trust, as you are delegating important responsibilities, and you will be bound by your Attorney-in-fact's actions as if they were your own.

Medical Care   **Do you want your Attorney-in-fact to authorize medical care for your minor child or children?**

( ) YES
( ) NO

Comment: Select "YES" if you want to authorize your Attorney-in-fact to make decisions about medical care for your children in your absence. Otherwise, select "NO".

This can be important if you are away from home and cannot be reached in the event of an emergency, or if you will be traveling while your children remain in another's care. Each child who is under the authority of the Attorney-in-fact must be listed.

Number Child   **How many children do you have?**

[Example: 2]

Comment: Enter this information in numbers.

Child Names   **Please enter the names of your child(ren).**

[Example: James C. Doe
Jennifer D. Doe]

Comment: Again be sure not to use abbreviations or nicknames. Each child who is under the authority of the Attorney-in-fact must be listed. If you have more than one child type each child's name on a separate line. Select <NEXT> to continue or [Enter] to move to the next line.

Real Estate   **Do you want your Attorney-in-fact to be able to sell, exchange, convey and/or mortgage your real estate?**

( ) YES
( ) NO

Comment: You can authorize your Attorney-in-fact to sell your real estate on your behalf and execute documents relating to the sale.

If you do not presently own, but subsequently acquire, real estate, you will want to prepare a new Power of Attorney to include a description of the real estate you acquire.

Real Describe   **Enter the legal description of the real estate covered by this Power of Attorney.**

Note: Do not follow the description with a period (.)

Comment: You must enter the legal description exactly as it appears in your deed. An inaccurate entry could prevent your Attorney-in-fact from acting on your behalf.

Personal Prop   **Do you want your Attorney-in-fact to be able to sell an item of your personal property?**

( ) YES
( ) NO

Comment: You can authorize your Attorney-in-fact to sell your personal property, such as a car, boat, trailer, motorcycle, etc.

Personal Desc   **Enter a description of the item of personal property to be sold by your Attorney-in-fact.**

Comment: Enter a complete and accurate description, including the type of property, style, color, manufacturer's serial number, etc.

It is important to clearly identify the item. Do not use terms which are so general that it could be interpreted to mean several items. Enter 'my 1989 4-door blue Toyota Camry, VIN 81J657823K' not 'my car'.

Expire?	**Do you want to set a specific termination date for this Power of Attorney?**

( ) YES
( ) NO

Comment: Select "YES" if you want to designate a specific termination date. Otherwise select "NO".

If you select a specific termination date, your Power of Attorney will expire upon the earlier of that date or your disability or incapacity. If you chose to create a Durable Power of Attorney, it will expire upon the date you select regardless of your prior disability or incapacity.

Expire Date	**Enter the date when you want this Power of Attorney to expire.**

[Example: 09/28/1992]

Comment: Unless Durable, your Power of Attorney will expire either on this date, or upon your disability or incapacity, whichever comes first. If Durable, it will expire on this date.

Execute Date	**Enter the date of execution of this Power of Attorney.**

[Example: 09/28/91]

Comment: This is the date when you will sign the Power of Attorney and have it witnessed and notarized. It may be a date in the future and not today's date.

If you own real estate, this Power of Attorney must also be filed in the office where deeds are recorded in the county where the real estate is located. If you chose to create a Durable Power of Attorney, your state may also require this Durable Power of Attorney to be filed with another public office.

Comment POA	**Your answers have indicated you do not want to create a Special Power of Attorney.**

Press [Esc] to return to the Main Menu.

Comment: Comment Only

Sample Document[1]

**DURABLE SPECIAL
POWER OF ATTORNEY**

NOTICE: THIS POWER OF ATTORNEY IS A LEGAL DOCUMENT, AND PROVIDES THE ATTORNEY-IN-FACT WITH BROAD POWERS OVER THE PRINCIPAL'S PROPERTY UNLESS LIMITED BY THE TERMS OF THE POWER OF ATTORNEY ITSELF. THE POWERS GIVEN TO THE ATTORNEY-IN-FACT MAY EXIST FOR AN UNLIMITED PERIOD OF TIME UNLESS LIMITED BY THE TERMS OF THE POWER OF ATTORNEY ITSELF. THE PRINCIPAL MAY REVOKE OR TERMINATE THIS POWER OF ATTORNEY AT ANY TIME. IF YOU NEED ADDITIONAL ADVICE ABOUT THIS POWER OF ATTORNEY, CONSULT WITH A LAWYER BEFORE SIGNING IT.

I, James R. Parker, of the County of King, State of Washington, hereby appoint Rachel P. Williams as my Attorney-in-fact, giving my Attorney-in-fact power to do the following specific act(s) only:

To make any and all arrangements that are appropriate and in the best interests of my children, Brian J. Parker and Karen L. Parker, for my children's personal care, support, maintenance, living arrangements, or medical, surgical or dental care;

To give consent in my name to any and all types of medical treatment or procedures, dental treatment or procedures or surgical procedures for my children;

To give consent in my name to the disclosure of any confidential or privileged communication or information related to the rendering of any care for my children, Brian J. Parker and Karen L. Parker;

To sign, acknowledge and deliver in my name any documents or instruments necessary to carry out any of the authority granted to my Attorney-in-fact by this Power of Attorney; and

To employ physicians, surgeons, nurses, dentists, or any other individual or institution necessary in order to render to my children, Brian J. Parker and Karen L. Parker, any of the types of care authorized by this Power of Attorney.

A photocopy of this instrument shall be deemed an original for all purposes.

---

[1] The sample document has been prepared and formatted for illustration purposes only. The actual document will print using the standard type style of your printer and the number of lines per page may differ.

This Power of Attorney shall not be affected by my disability or incapacity. It is my intent that this instrument be construed as a Durable Power of Attorney. If state law requires that a Power of Attorney be filed in any public office in order to be a legally accepted Power of Attorney, I direct my Attorney-in-fact to file an executed copy of this instrument in such public office.

This Power of Attorney shall terminate on January 1st, 1992.

If any part of this Power of Attorney is held to be invalid under any law, the remainder of this instrument shall not be affected by such invalidity.

IN WITNESS WHEREOF, I have executed this Power of Attorney on October 15th, 1991.

James R. Parker,
Principal

ATTESTATION

We hereby certify that this Power of Attorney was signed, declared and published by James R. Parker as his Power of Attorney on this day, in our presence and in the presence of each other, and we sign our names below as Witnesses in his presence, at his request and in the presence of each other on October 15th, 1991.

Resides at

Witness 1 Signature   Street Address

Witness 1 Name (Printed)   City, State, Zip

Resides at

Witness 2 Signature   Street Address

Witness 2 Name (Printed)   City, State, Zip

State of Washington   )
) ss.
County of King   )

   On this _____ day of _____, 19___, before me, the undersigned, a Notary Public in and for the State and County named above, personally appeared James R. Parker, who is known to me personally as the Principal described in and who executed the above Power of Attorney, and, after first being sworn, declared this instrument as his free act and deed, and signed it in my presence.

   Subscribed and sworn to before me this _____ day of _____, 19___ .

My Commission Expires:

_____ _____
             NOTARY PUBLIC

         (SEAL)

Revocation of Power of Attorney

Document Summary

Home Lawyer's Revocation of Power of Attorney is used by one person (the Principal) to revoke the power previously given to another (the Attorney-in-fact). A Revocation may be necessary for a variety of reasons -- the Principal wants to appoint a new Attorney-in-fact, the Attorney-in-fact cannot continue to serve, or the relationship between the parties may have changed significantly.

Whatever the reason, certain steps should be taken to help ensure that the Revocation takes effect. If the Power of Attorney being revoked was recorded in any government office, the Revocation should also be recorded in the same office. A copy of the Revocation should be sent to the Attorney-in-fact by certified mail, return receipt requested. The receipt will help serve as proof in the unlikely event the Attorney-in-fact tries to act on your behalf after the revocation takes place. If possible, you should also hand deliver a copy to the Attorney-in-fact.

If you know the identities of other parties the Attorney-in-fact has dealt with on your behalf, you should also mail copies of the Revocation to them. This will serve as notice to them that the Attorney-in-fact is no longer your representative, and that you will not be bound by his or her actions.

Questions and Comments

Note: The following describes <u>every</u> question for the Revocation of Power of Attorney. However, during the Question and Answer session, the program will display only those questions relevant to your personal situation.

Revoke Name   **What is your full legal name?**

[Example: Jonathan A. Doe]

Comment: You should enter your name exactly as it appears in the Power of Attorney you wish to revoke.

Male/Female   **Choose your gender.**

( ) Male
( ) Female

Comment: This choice controls gender replacement within the document.

County Name   **In what county do you live?**

[Example: Mason]

Comment: In Louisiana, enter your Parish here. In Alaska, enter your Judicial District here.

County Type   **Select the appropriate designation.**

[Example: County]

Note: In Louisiana select Parish, in Alaska select Judicial District, and for most other states select county.

( ) County
( ) Parish
( ) Judicial District
( ) Other

Comment: Select County, Parish or Judicial District. Select Other if none of these apply.

Other Territory   **Please enter the designation for your location.**

Comment: Be sure to capitalize the first letter.

State   **Enter the state where you live.**

[Example: IL]

Comment: Use the two-letter abbreviation for your state.

Revoke Atty   **Enter the full legal name of your Attorney-in-fact (the person you designated to act in your behalf in the Power of Attorney you wish to revoke).**

[Example: Susan S. Alexander]

Comment: You should enter this name exactly as it appears in the Power of Attorney you wish to revoke.

POA Date   **Enter the date of the Power of Attorney you wish to revoke.**

[Example: 09/28/1991]

Comment: This is the date of execution of the Power of Attorney you want to revoke (cancel).

Sample Document[1]

REVOCATION OF
POWER OF ATTORNEY

I, James A. Moore, of the County of King, State of Washington, hereby revoke the Power of Attorney given to John G. Williams on October 20th, 1991, and I declare that Power of Attorney to be null and void. A copy of said Power of Attorney marked "REVOKED" is attached to this revocation and is incorporated in this revocation by reference.

Dated this ____ day of _____, 19__.

_____
James A. Moore

ATTESTATION

We hereby certify that on this ____ day of _____, 19__, we witnessed James A. Moore sign and execute this instrument, declaring and publishing it as his Revocation of a Power of Attorney, in our presence and in the presence of each other. We believe James A. Moore to be of sound mind, under no compulsion or duress, and we sign our names below as Witnesses in his presence, at his request and in the presence of each other, this ____ day of _____, 19__.

Resides at

_____   _____
Witness 1 Signature   Street Address

_____   _____
Witness 1 Name (Printed)   City, State, Zip

Resides at

_____   _____
Witness 2 Signature   Street Address

_____   _____
Witness 2 Name (Printed)   City, State, Zip

---

[1] The sample document has been prepared and formatted for illustration purposes only. The actual document will print using the standard type style of your printer and the number of lines per page may differ.

State of Washington   )
) ss.

County of King   )

      On this _____ day of _____, 19 __ , before me, the undersigned, a Notary Public in and for the State and County named above, personally appeared James A. Moore, who is known to me to be the Principal described in and who executed the above Revocation of a Power of Attorney, and after first being sworn, declared this instrument as his free act and deed, and signed it in my presence.

Subscribed and sworn to before me this _____ day of _____, 19 __ .

My Commission Expires:

_____

                        _____
                        NOTARY PUBLIC

              (SEAL)

Employment Agreement

Document Summary

Home Lawyer's Employment Agreement is a contract between a business and an individual who will serve as an employee of the business. Terms included in the Employment Agreement cover issues such as salary, bonuses, expenses and fringe benefits. Provision can also be made for sick leave and vacation time.

An Employment Agreement can be helpful for both the employer and employee, and eliminate confusion about the responsibilities each has toward the other. Unless an employee has a written agreement, the employee is usually considered an "employee at will," and can be terminated for any reason or no reason at all.

Every state has laws regarding the relationship between employers and employees. In addition, the federal Department of Labor is authorized to enforce federal laws regarding wages, hours, and other employment issues. Home Lawyer's Employment Agreement contains a provision which permits the remainder of the contract to remain in effect in the event one or more provisions are invalid because of any law.

Laws governing the relationship of employers and their employees vary widely, and are subject to different interpretations. If you have any questions regarding the provisions of Home Lawyer's Employment Agreement as they apply in your state, we recommend that you consult with an attorney before signing the agreement. Your state or local bar association can provide you with a referral to an attorney who can assist you.

Questions and Comments

Note: The following describes <u>every</u> question for the Employment Agreement. However, during the Question and Answer session, the program will display only those questions relevant to your personal situation.

Corp Name   **Enter the employer's name.**

[Example: ABC Corporation]

Comment: If the employer uses a fictitious business name (D/B/A), enter the employer's actual name, D/B/A, and the fictitious name (e.g. Jim Johnson, D/B/A, Johnson Delivery Service).

Corp Business   **What is the form of the employer's business?**

[Example: corporation
*   a partnership]*

( ) An Individual
( ) A Partnership
( ) A Corporation
( ) A Sole Proprietorship

Comment: Select the form of business (e.g. sole proprietorship, corporation, individual or partnership). Use Advisor and choose Glossary of Terms for brief explanations of these terms.

Corp Address   **Enter the street address of the employer.**

[Example: 1270 Anystreet, Suite 135]

Comment: If the street address is more than one line, use commas to separate each part. The address is usually the place where the job is. It may not be the headquarters of the corporation.

Corp City   **Enter the city of the employer.**

[Example: Cleveland]

Comment: It is not necessary to add a comma at the end of the name of the city.

Corp State	**Enter the state of the employer.**

[Example: OH]

Comment: Use the two-letter state abbreviation.

Corp Zip   **Enter the zip code of the employer.**

[Example: 98136-1351]

Comment: Use the nine-digit zip code when possible. The nine-digit zip code helps speed mail delivery. The five-digit zip code is required on most documents and for most mailing addresses.

Employee   **Enter the name of the employee.**

[Example: Mary S. Smith]

Comment: Do not use any nicknames or abbreviations. The name must be the legal name, not the social name.

Male/Female   **Choose the appropriate gender for the employee.**

( ) Male
( ) Female

Press [Enter] or select <NEXT> to move to the next question.

Employ Addr   **Enter the street address of the employee.**

[Example: 1270 Anystreet, Suite 135]

Comment: If the street address is more than one line, use commas to separate each part.

Employ City   **Enter the city of the employee.**

[Example: Cleveland]

Comment: It is not necessary to add a comma at the end of the name of the city.

Employ State **Enter the state of the employee.**

[Example: OH]

Comment: Use the two-letter state abbreviation.

Employ Zip **Enter the zip code of the employee.**

[Example: 98136-1352]

Comment: Use the nine-digit zip code when possible. The nine-digit zip code helps speed mail delivery. The five-digit zip code is required on most documents and for most mailing addresses.

Employ Term **Enter the length of time for which the employment agreement will run.**

[Example: one year]

Comment: You may agree upon as long or short a term as both parties wish. Many employment agreements are for a term of one year.

Notice **How much notice must be given for either party to terminate the employment agreement?**

[Example: thirty days]

Comment: You may agree upon as much or as little notice as both parties wish before the employment agreement can be canceled. The length of the notice is often arranged at the time of employment.

Annual Salary **Enter the annual salary the employee will receive.**

[Example: 50,000.00]

Note: The program automatically adds commas where necessary.

Comment: Enter the annual salary in numbers. Use the right arrow key or decimal point to add cents.

Vacation   **Enter the amount of paid vacation time in weeks the employee will receive annually.**

[Example: 2]

Comment: Vacation time is indicated in weeks. Use numbers, not words, to show how much leave the employer will pay each year. Paid vacation is normally in addition to the usual holidays.

Paid Sick Days   **Will the employee receive paid sick days?**

( ) YES
( ) NO

Comment: This document provides for sick days with full compensation.

Sick Days   **Enter the number of paid sick days the employee will receive annually.**

[Example: 5]

Comment: This document provides sick leave in days. The number is the maximum number of days the employee may take annually.

Reviews   **Will there be scheduled performance reviews?**

( ) YES
( ) NO

Comment: Press [Enter] or select <NEXT> to move to the next question.

Review Days   **Enter the length of time between each performance review.**

[Example: six months]

Comment: This is the number of days, weeks or months after the first day of employment that will pass before the first review. Subsequent reviews will follow at equivalent intervals.

Sample Document[1]

EMPLOYMENT AGREEMENT

This Agreement is made by and between ABC Corporation, a corporation located at 3490 Industrial Parkway, Cleveland, Ohio 44112, and Mary K. Jackson, an individual residing at 3492 Rosewood Drive, Lakewood, Ohio 44193.

WHEREAS Mary K. Jackson and ABC Corporation desire to create an employment arrangement under the terms and conditions contained in this Agreement;

NOW, THEREFORE, in consideration of the foregoing, and the following covenants and promises, and for other good and valuable consideration, ABC Corporation and Mary K. Jackson agree as follows:

1.   Employment. ABC Corporation employs Mary K. Jackson, who accepts such employment. ABC Corporation and Mary K. Jackson revoke, terminate and void any prior written or oral employment agreements.

2.   Term.
2.1 This Agreement shall be for a period of one year beginning on the date of this Agreement, unless terminated in accordance with some other provision of this Agreement.
2.2 The Agreement may be terminated by either Party upon thirty days' written notice to the other.

3.   Compensation.
3.1 For all services rendered under this Agreement by Mary K. Jackson, ABC Corporation shall pay Mary K. Jackson a basic gross salary of forty-five thousand dollars ($45,000.00) per year, payable in periodic installments in a manner consistent with the accounting practices adopted by ABC Corporation.
3.2 Mary K. Jackson may receive bonuses in addition to the compensation stated above when and as determined by ABC Corporation.
3.3 ABC Corporation agrees to pay Mary K. Jackson her full basic salary during the term of this Agreement, so long as she is willing and able to perform her duties and obligations and has not defaulted under this Agreement.

4.   Duties and Responsibilities.
4.1 Mary K. Jackson shall devote substantially all her business time and attention to the business of ABC Corporation. The expenditure of reasonable time for personal or outside business, charitable and professional activities shall not constitute a breach of this Agreement if such activities do not materially interfere with Mary K. Jackson's performance of her duties and obligations, as solely determined by ABC

---

[1] The sample document has been prepared and formatted for illustration purposes only. The actual document will print using the standard type style of your printer and the number of lines per page may differ.

Corporation. Mary K. Jackson agrees to place her duties to ABC Corporation above all other activities and will abandon or curtail outside activities if so directed by ABC Corporation if in its opinion there exists a conflict or other reasonable grounds for abandoning or curtailing such activities.

4.2 At Mary K. Jackson's own cost and expense, Mary K. Jackson must use her own automobile for professional and other business purposes. Mary K. Jackson shall be entitled to standard mileage allowance, the amount to be determined by reference to Internal Revenue Service Guidelines, for travel conducted on behalf of ABC Corporation.

5. Authority and Powers of ABC Corporation. ABC Corporation shall have the power to direct, control and supervise Mary K. Jackson's duties and the manner of and time for performing said duties.

6. Working Facilities and Expenses.

6.1 ABC Corporation will furnish Mary K. Jackson with facilities and services suitable for the performance of Mary K. Jackson's duties and obligations under this Agreement.

6.2 In accordance with the established policies of ABC Corporation, Mary K. Jackson may be reimbursed for reasonable expenses related to the performance of her duties including (but not limited to): automobile and transportation expenses; entertainment expenses; costs of maintaining facilities in her home; educational expenses incurred to maintain or improve her professional skills; expenses of membership in civic groups, clubs, professional societies and fraternal organizations; and all other items of reasonable and necessary professional expenses incurred by Mary K. Jackson in the performance of her duties as an employee.

7. Health and Insurance Plans: Fringe Benefits. Mary K. Jackson may be entitled to participate in any plans or agreements regarding retirement, health, disability, life insurance, and other related fringe benefits provided by ABC Corporation, in accordance with the terms and conditions of each.

8. Vacations and Other Time Off.

8.1 Mary K. Jackson shall be entitled to an annual vacation of two (2) week(s), with full basic salary, and at times approved by ABC Corporation.

8.2 Mary K. Jackson shall be entitled to further additional time (with full basic salary) for attendance at meetings, conventions, seminars and/or post-graduate courses reasonably related to the performance of her duties, as approved in advance by ABC Corporation.

8.3 Mary K. Jackson shall be entitled to five (5) days sick leave with full basic salary, as approved by ABC Corporation. No additional compensation shall be paid in the event Mary K. Jackson fails to use the allotted sick days. No additional sick leave or other leave days are contemplated by this Agreement, except as described in this paragraph.

9.   Miscellaneous.
        9.1 This Agreement may only be amended by a written document signed by Mary K. Jackson and ABC Corporation.
        9.2 No provision of this Agreement shall be affected by the invalidity of any other provision.
        9.3 This Agreement shall be interpreted in accordance with the laws of Ohio.

_____   _____
Date   For ABC Corporation

_____   _____
Date   Witness

_____   _____
Date   Mary K. Jackson

_____   _____
Date   Witness

Independent Contractor Agreement

Document Summary

Home Lawyer's Independent Contractor Agreement is a contract between a business (or individual) and an individual who will serve as an independent contractor or consultant.

An independent contractor can include someone you have hired to build a fence or add a deck to your home. For small businesses, it can be used for someone such as a computer programmer.

An independent contractor is not an employee of the business he or she serves. As a result, the independent contractor is not entitled to any of the employee benefits the business may provide, and the independent contractor is responsible for paying any income taxes, workers' compensation, unemployment insurance, and social security taxes that may result from his or her work. On the positive side, the independent contractor is not subject to the control of the business in matters such as where or when work should be performed.

Home Lawyer's Independent Contractor Agreement gives the parties wide latitude in describing the consultant's duties. As a result, it is important to be as specific as possible in detailing the nature of the work to be done.

Because state laws regarding independent contractors vary and are subject to different interpretations, if any provision of Home Lawyer's Independent Contractor Agreement is found to be invalid, the remainder of the agreement remains in effect.

If either the business or the consultant is unsure of any of the provisions of the Independent Contractor Agreement, we recommend consulting with an attorney before signing the agreement. Your state or local bar association can provide you with a referral to an attorney who can assist you.

Questions and Comments

Note: The following describes every question for the Independent Contractor Agreement. However, during the Question and Answer session, the program will display only those questions relevant to your personal situation.

Corp Name

Enter the employer's name.

[Example: ABC Corporation]

Comment: If the employer uses a fictitious business name (D/B/A), enter the employer's actual name, D/B/A, and the fictitious name (e.g. Jim Johnson, D/B/A, Johnson Delivery Service).

Corp Business

What is the form of the employer's business?

[Example: corporation
a partnership]

( ) An Individual
( ) A Partnership
( ) A Corporation
( ) A Sole Proprietorship

Comment: Select the form of business (e.g. sole proprietorship, corporation, individual or partnership). Use Advisor and choose Glossary of Terms for brief explanations of these terms.

Corp Address

Enter the street address of the employer.

[Example: 1270 Anystreet, Suite 135]

Comment: If the street address is more than one line, use commas to separate each part. The address is usually the place where the job is. It may not be the headquarters of the corporation.

Corp City

Enter the city of the employer.

[Example: Cleveland]

Comment: It is not necessary to add a comma at the end of the name of the city.

Corp State	**Enter the state of the employer.**

[Example: OH]

Comment: Use the two-letter state abbreviation.

Corp Zip   **Enter the zip code of the employer.**

[Example: 98136-1351]

Comment: Use the nine-digit zip code when possible. The nine-digit zip code helps speed mail delivery. The five-digit zip code is required on most documents and for most mailing addresses.

Consultant   **Enter the name of the independent contractor/consultant.**

[Example: Mary S. Smith]

Comment: Do not use any nicknames or abbreviations. The name must be the legal name, not the social name.

Male/Female Cn   **Choose the gender which fits the consultant.**

( ) Male
( ) Female

Comment: This choice controls gender replacements within the document. Select <NEXT> or press [Enter] to move to the next question.

Consult Addr   **Enter the street address of the consultant.**

[Example: 1270 Anystreet, Suite 135]

Comment: If the street address is more than one line, use commas to separate each part.

Consult City   **Enter the city of the consultant.**

[Example: Cleveland]

Comment: It is not necessary to add a comma at the end of the name of the city. Use the name of the community as named by the United States Post Office.

Consult State   **Enter the state of the consultant.**

[Example: OH]

Comment: Use the two-letter state abbreviation.

Consult Zip   **Enter the zip code of the consultant.**

[Example: 98136-1351]

Comment: Use the nine-digit zip code when possible. The nine-digit zip code helps speed mail delivery. The five-digit zip code is required on most documents and for most mailing addresses.

Duty Desc   **Do you want to describe the specific duties of the consultant?**

( ) YES
( ) NO

Comment: Select "YES" if a description of the consultant's duties is to be included in this document. Otherwise, select "NO".

Consult Duty   **Enter a description of the consultant's duties.**

Note: Begin each duty with the word "to"
and separate the duties with
semicolons.

Comment: You may enter up to 12 lines of duties. Do not include a period at the end. Select <NEXT> to move to the next question.

Include in the description all special arrangements which you wish to document. This is the place to note unusual working conditions, plans for the consultant to use his or her own equipment or other circumstances surrounding the consultant relationship. Example: To program the IBM 36 by automating customer service intake data systems; to document customer service programs; and to develop reference materials for the user.

Consult Start   **Enter the starting date of this Agreement.**

[Example: 09/28/91]

Comment: The starting date indicates the date you expect the consulting arrangement to begin.

Consult End   **Enter the ending date of this Agreement.**

[Example: 09/28/1992]

Comment: This date is the date you expect the consulting arrangement to end. It may be extended by mutual agreement.

Type Pay   **How will the consultant be paid?**

( ) By the hour
( ) By the week
( ) By the job

Comment: Enter the letter of your choice. Press [Enter] or select <NEXT> to move to the next question.

How Pay Conslt   **When will the consultant be paid?**

( ) Weekly
( ) Twice Per Month
( ) Upon Completion
( ) Other

Comment: This describes when the consultant will receive payment for his or her performance.

When Pay Desc   **Enter the description of when the consultant will be paid.**

[Example: one-half the amount before
the service is performed
and the balance upon
completion]

Comment: Begin with a lower case letter and do not end with a period (.). Select <NEXT> to move to the next question.

Pay Rate   **Enter the pay rate the consultant will receive.**

[Example: 10.00 (if hourly)
500.00 (if weekly)
1,500.00 (if upon completion)]

Comment: Enter the pay rate in numbers, using dollars and cents. Use the right arrow key or decimal point to add cents. The program automatically adds commas where necessary.

Non Compete   **Do you want the consultant bound not to compete?**

( ) YES
( ) NO

Comment: In business consulting situations, you may want to prohibit the consultant from working with a competitor while servicing your account.

State laws vary on the enforceability of clauses restricting an independent consultant's right to work for a competitor. You should consult with an attorney or contact your local library for more information about the law in your state.

Confidential   **Should the consultant be bound to keep information regarding your job confidential?**

( ) YES
( ) NO

Comment: Select "YES" if the consultant will be exposed to valuable sales or financial information to be kept confidential. Otherwise, select "NO".

Expense   **Do you want to reimburse the consultant for reasonable expenses relating to this job?**

( ) YES
( ) NO

Comment: Select "YES" to entitle the consultant to reimbursement for all "reasonable and necessary" expenses incurred as a result of duties performed. Otherwise, select "NO".

Sample Document[1]

INDEPENDENT CONSULTANT AGREEMENT

THIS AGREEMENT ("Agreement") is made by ABC Corporation, a corporation at 4590 Industrial Parkway, Cleveland, Ohio 44112 ("Employer") and Martha B. Smithson, at 1248 Oakwood Drive, Lakewood, Ohio 44156 ("Consultant").

WHEREAS, Martha B. Smithson has expertise in providing the services sought by ABC Corporation; and

WHEREAS, ABC Corporation wishes to utilize Martha B. Smithson's services and abilities during the term of this Agreement, and Martha B. Smithson is willing to offer such services upon the terms and conditions contained in this Agreement;

NOW THEREFORE, in consideration of the promises contained herein, the parties agree as follows:

1. Engagement and Duties. During the term of this Agreement, ABC Corporation hereby engages Martha B. Smithson and Martha B. Smithson hereby agrees to serve ABC Corporation, as an independent consultant. Martha B. Smithson shall be available to work at reasonable times and for reasonable periods of time to perform the services required by ABC Corporation. Consultant's duties shall be as follows: To program the IBM 36 automating customer service intake systems; to document the customer service programs; and to develop reference materials for the user.

2. Term. This Agreement shall begin on October 1st, 1991 and shall terminate on April 1st, 1992.

3. Compensation. For all services rendered by Martha B. Smithson under this Agreement, Martha B. Smithson shall be paid at a rate of fifty dollars ($50.00) per hour, payable weekly on each Friday. Martha B. Smithson's relationship shall be that of an independent consultant and ABC Corporation shall not withhold taxes or Social Security payments from any sum paid to Martha B. Smithson under this Agreement.

4. Specific Performance. The parties acknowledge that the obligations of ABC Corporation and of Martha B. Smithson under this Agreement are incapable of valuation with any reasonable degree of certainty. In the event that either party should fail to fulfill any of the obligations of this Agreement, the other party may bring an action to enforce specific performance of all obligations under this Agreement. This remedy shall not exclude the availability of any other remedy permitted by law.

---

[1] The sample document has been prepared and formatted for illustration purposes only. The actual document will print using the standard type style of your printer and the number of lines per page may differ.

5. Miscellaneous. This Agreement shall inure to the benefit of and be binding upon the parties and their respective successors, assigns, heirs and personal representatives and, except as specifically provided herein, neither party may make any assignment of this Agreement or any interest therein without the prior written consent of the other party. It is understood and agreed that ABC Corporation shall have the right to assign this Agreement to any successor to all or substantially all of its assets and business by dissolution, merger, consolidation, transfer of assets or otherwise, or to any direct or indirect subsidiary of ABC Corporation.

The laws of the State of Ohio shall govern this Agreement.

If any provision of this Agreement is invalid or inoperative under law, the remaining provisions of this Agreement shall continue in full force and effect.

This Agreement contains the entire agreement of the parties, and supersedes any and all previous agreements they may have made, whether orally or in writing.

IN WITNESS WHEREOF, the parties hereto have set their hands.

_____   _____
Date   ABC Corporation

                                    _____
                                    Witness

_____   _____
Date   Martha B. Smithson

                                    _____
                                    Witness

Offer of Employment Letter

Document Summary

The Offer of Employment letter allows you to specify the position being offered, an annual salary, a starting date and other details of the position being offered. You should note that once the offer is accepted, this letter could be viewed as a legally binding agreement between the employer and the new employee. If you want a more detailed description of the employment arrangement, you should use Home Lawyer's Employment Agreement in addition to this letter.

Questions and Comments

Note: The following describes <u>every</u> question for the Offer of Employment Letter. However, during the Question and Answer session, the program will display only those questions relevant to your personal situation.

Corp Name Enter the employer's name.

[Example: ABC Corporation]

Comment: If the employer uses a fictitious business name (D/B/A), enter the employer's actual name, D/B/A, and the fictitious name (e.g. Jim Johnson, D/B/A, Johnson Delivery Service).

Corp Address Enter the street address of the employer.

[Example: 1270 Anystreet, Suite 135]

Comment: If the street address is more than one line, use commas to separate each part. The address is usually the place where the job is. It may not be the headquarters of the corporation.

Corp CSZ Enter the city, state and zip code of the employer.

[Example: Seattle, WA 98139]

Comment: Use the name of the community as named by the United States Post Office. Do not use the name of a real estate sub-division unless it is used as a Post Office address.

Letter Date **Enter the date you intend to send this letter.**

[Example: 09/28/91]

Comment: Use the MM/DD/YY format. It is not necessary to spell out the date.

Employ Sal **Enter the courtesy title of the employee to be used in the salutation.**

[Example: Mr., Mrs., Ms., or Dr.]

Comment: See the examples provided as a guide.

Employ First **Enter the first name of the employee.**

[Example: Mary]

Comment: Do not use any abbreviations or nicknames.

Middle Init **Enter the middle initial (optional).**

[Example: B.]

Comment: Use of the initial is optional. Include the period after the initial.

Employ Last **Enter the last name of the employee.**

[Example: Smith]

Comment: Do not use any nicknames or abbreviations.

Employ Addr **Enter the street address of the employee.**

[Example: 1270 Anystreet, Suite 135]

Comment: If the street address is more than one line, use commas to separate each part.

Employ CSZ   **Enter the employee's city, state and zip code.**

[Example: Seattle, WA 98139]

Comment: Use the name of the community as named by the United States Post Office. Do not use the name of a real estate sub-division unless it is used as a Post Office address.

Job Title   **Enter the new employee's job title.**

[Example: Administrative Assistant]

Comment: Spell out the complete job title. Do not use abbreviations. The job title should be the one agreed upon between the employer and the new employee.

Start Date Emp   **Enter the start date of the new employee.**

[Example: 09/28/91]

Comment: Use the MM/DD/YY format. It is not necessary to spell out the date.

Start Time Emp   **Enter the time at which the new employee should report on the first day.**

[Example: 8:00 a.m.]

Comment: Enter the complete time of day (for example, 9:00 a.m.). Be sure to include a.m. or p.m. as appropriate.

Supervisor   **Enter the name and job title of the person to whom the new employee will report.**

[Example: James Smith, General Manager]

Comment: Do not use nicknames or abbreviations. Use the legal name of the supervisor, and his or her organization title.

Annual Salary **Enter the annual salary the employee will receive.**

[Example: 50,000.00]

Note: The program automatically adds commas where necessary.

Comment: Enter the annual salary in numbers. Use the right arrow key or decimal point to add cents.

Pay Days **Enter the company's pay period and pay days.**

[Example: monthly, on the first day of each month]

Comment: State the company policy carefully and clearly. For example, use monthly, on the first day of each month or twice a month, on the 15th and the last day of each month.

Contract **Will a contract follow the acceptance of the terms of this agreement?**

( ) YES
( ) NO

Comment: A contract allows you to expand on the terms outlined in this Offer of Employment.

Although the Offer of Employment gives the outline of the terms and conditions under which the employee will work, you may choose to elaborate on these terms through an Employment Agreement. If you choose this option, you may use Home Lawyer's Employment Agreement as the contract.

Preparer **Enter the name of the person to sign the letter.**

[Example: Anne M. Thomas]

Comment: Type the name as he or she will sign the letter. It is not necessary to use the legal name of the preparer, but it is preferred.

Letterhead   **Will you be printing this letter on letterhead?**

( ) YES
( ) NO

Comment: Selecting "NO" will cause the program to print your return address at the top of the document. Selecting "YES" will add blank lines to accommodate letterhead paper.

Sample Document[1]

ABC Corporation
4394 Industrial Parkway
Cleveland, OH 44111

October 1, 1991

Mr. James T. Jackson
4599 Oak St.
Cleveland, OH 44111

Subject: Employment

Dear Mr. Jackson:

On behalf of ABC Corporation ("The Company"), I am pleased to extend to you an offer of employment to work with us as Assistant Manager. Your duties will commence at 8:00 a.m. on November 1st, 1991.

You will work directly for Janet Smith, General Manager, and will be responsible for those duties outlined in your job description. You will be compensated at the rate of thirty-five thousand dollars ($35,000.00) per year, paid twice a month, on the 15th and last day of each month. In addition to the above, you are eligible for the standard fringe benefit package offered by the company. You will also have an opportunity to participate in any optional benefits which may be offered.

If the above conforms with your understanding of our agreement, please sign both copies of this letter agreement and return one to me in the enclosed envelope.

Upon acceptance of this letter agreement, an employment contract will follow.

Allow me to be the first to offer my congratulations to you on this offer of employment. I sincerely hope that you accept it and look forward to working closely with you in the near future.

Sincerely,

By: Anne M. Thomas
For: ABC Corporation

I agree to the above terms and accept employment with you.

Date _____

_____
James T. Jackson

---

[1] The sample document has been prepared and formatted for illustration purposes only. The actual document will print using the standard type style of your printer and the number of lines per page may differ.

Promissory Note

Document Summary

"Neither a Lender or Borrower Be" goes the old saying. But in today's credit-driven society, the ability to borrow money is valuable. As a Lender, a promissory note provides protection against questions that may later arise over the amount of money loaned, whether or not interest is being charged, and when amounts are to be repaid.

In the event the person who has borrowed money dies prior to repayment, a promissory note can be presented to the executor of the estate to receive payment even after his or her death.

Clearly stating all the terms regarding interest and repayment is equally important to the Borrower. If the Borrower repays part of the debt, the note will protect him or her for any unearned interest that the Lender may claim is due.

Home Lawyer's Promissory Note obligates one party (the Maker) to pay money to another (the Payee). A Promissory Note is used when the Payee has loaned money or something else of value to the Maker and repayment is to be made according to specified terms. For example, you have a good friend or relative who has asked you to help him out financially. It would be a good idea for both parties involved to have the repayment plan spelled out in writing.

Home Lawyer's Promissory Note provides several repayment options, including no-interest payment and payment on demand. Choose the one that best serves the needs of the parties.

A Promissory Note that requires the payment of interest must comply with the usury laws in the state where it is made. Usury laws establish a maximum interest rate that may be charged. A Promissory Note that charges an excessive rate of interest may be found null and void. You can contact your county law librarian or an attorney for information about the usury laws in your state.

Keep in mind that Home Lawyer's Promissory Note creates an unsecured debt. If the Maker of the Note defaults, the Payee will have to obtain a court judgment in order to collect the unpaid amount due. If the Maker files bankruptcy, the Payee may be unable to enforce the Note. There are other kinds of documents (called security agreements) that can provide additional protection to the Payee. An attorney can help you prepare and file a security agreement if you think you need one.

Special Considerations

SCHEDULE OF PAYMENTS

Date	Item	Amount	Balance

Instructions to the Holder: This schedule will help you keep track of the loan. The first entry is the loan. Then, each month, make an entry for the interest. You can calculate the monthly interest by multiplying (1/12) x (Interest Rate) x (Current Balance). Then add it to the Current Balance. In the next entry after that, subtract the payment made. See, for example, this eight percent loan for $12,000.00, with the following transactions:

(For Example Only)

1/1/89	Loan made at 8%	$12,000.00	$12,000.00
2/1/89	Interest for Jan. (1/12) x (.08) x (12,000) =	80.00	12,080.00
2/1/89	Payment of $211.00	<211.00>	11,869.00
3/1/89	Interest for Feb. (1/12) x (.08) x (11,869) =	79.13	11,948.13
3/1/89	Payment of $211.00	<211.00>	11,737.13
4/1/89	Interest for March (1/12) x (.08) x (11,737.13) =	78.24	11,815.37
	Etc.	Etc.	Etc.

Questions and Comments

Note: The following describes every question for the Promissory Note. However, during the Question and Answer session, the program will display only those questions relevant to your personal situation.

No. Makers **How many Makers (Borrower) are there for this note?**

( ) One Maker
( ) Two Makers
( ) Three Makers

Comment: The program allows you to enter the names of up to three Makers. The Maker of a promissory note is the person obligated to pay it. This is typically the Borrower.

Print a worksheet for the promissory note after answering Yes or No to charging interest on the note. This will allow you to see those questions involved (a) if there is interest in your note; or (b) if there is no interest in your note.

To print a worksheet, under the Edit Menu, select Print Worksheet. Using your arrow keys, make the desired selection (Short Form or Long Form) and press [Enter]. Select the Printer Output (Printer or File) and press [Enter].

Maker 1   **Enter the full legal name of the Maker (Borrower) of this note.**

[Example: Jonathan A. Doe]

Comment: Do not use any nicknames or abbreviations. The name must be the legal name, not the social name.

Maker 2   **Enter the full legal name of the second Maker (Borrower) of this note.**

[Example: Mary B. Doe]

Comment: Do not use any nicknames or abbreviations. The name must be the legal name, not the social name.

Maker 3   **Enter the full legal name of the third Maker (Borrower) of this note.**

[Example: Paul C. Doe]

Comment: Do not use any nicknames or abbreviations. The name must be the legal name, not the social name.

No. Payees   **How many Payees (Lender) are there for this note? You may have up to two.**

( ) One Payee
( ) Two Payees

Comment: The Payee is the person to whom payment on the note is made. This is typically the Lender.

Payee1   **Enter the full legal name of the Payee (Lender) of this note.**

[Example: Harry A. Hanson]

Comment: Do not use any nicknames or abbreviations. The name must be the legal name, not the social name.

Payee 2   **Enter the full legal name of the second Payee (Lender) of this note.**

[Example: Martha B. Hanson]

Comment: Do not use any nicknames or abbreviations. The name must be the legal name, not the social name.

Principal   **What is the principal amount of this note?**

[Example: 1,000.00]

Note: The program will automatically add commas where necessary.

Comment: The principal is the amount of money owed not including interest. Enter the full amount in dollars and cents. Use the right arrow key or decimal point to add cents.

Interest   **Will interest be charged on this Note?**

( ) YES
( ) NO

Comment: Some states have usury laws which limit the amount of interest that may be charged on a debt.

Interest Rate   **What is the interest rate (%) on this note?**

[Example: 10.5]

Comment: This refers to the annual interest rate charged while money is owed. For example, 10 would equal 10 percent per year.

Home Lawyer will allow a maximum of 99.99% interest to be charged on a Promissory Note.

Some states have usury laws which limit the amount of interest that may be charged on a debt. Please check your state law.

How To Pay   **How will principal and interest payments be made on this note?**

( ) Equal monthly installments
( ) Payment in full on demand
( ) Interest monthly
( ) Minimum monthly payment
( ) Pay in full by date

Comment: Make your selection. Press <ENTER> or select <NEXT> to move to the next question.

This program gives you several options for structuring payments of loans which bear interest.

Equal Monthly Installments specifies that the Maker (Borrower) is to pay the same amount each month for the period the money is owed.

Payment in Full on Demand specifies that no payment is due until the holder (Lender) sends a written notice (demand) for payment.

Interest monthly specifies that payments of interest only are due until a specified date at which time the entire unpaid amount will be due.

Minimum monthly specifies that the Maker (Borrower) will make payments equal to or greater than a specified amount.

Pay in Full by Date specifies that the Maker (Borrower) is to pay the entire amount at a future date.

Installment   **Enter the total number of monthly installments.**

[Example: 12, 24, 36, etc.]

Comment: Installments are periodic payments (e.g. monthly) of equal amounts. Enter the figure in numbers. Do not use '0'. Calculate the number of payments based on twelve per year.

Install Amt1   **Enter the amount of each installment.**

[Example: 100.00]

Use the right arrow key or decimal point to add cents.

Comment: Enter the figure in numbers. This amount is due the first day of each month. The language of the note makes any unpaid interest and principal due on the date of the last payment.

Due Dat Prncpl   **Enter the date when payment of the principal and any unpaid interest is due.**

[Example: 09/28/1991]

Comment: Maker will make interest only payments on the first of each month until this date. On this date, the principal and accrued interest are due.

Month Payment   **Enter the minimum monthly payment to be made.**

[Example: 135.00]

Note: The program automatically adds commas where necessary.

Comment: This is the smallest amount Payee will accept each month. Enter this amount in numbers.

Use the right arrow key or decimal point to add cents.

Due Date Bal   **Enter the date when payment of the principal and any unpaid interest is due.**

[Example: 09/28/1991]

Comment: Maker's monthly payments will be credited first against interest and then against principal. On this date, the balance of the principal and any accrued interest are due.

How Pay   **How will principal payments be made on this note?**

( ) Equal monthly installments
( ) Payment in full by date
( ) Payment in full on demand

Comment: Make your selection. Press <ENTER> or select <NEXT> to move to the next question.

This program gives you several options for structuring payments of loans which bear no interest.

Equal Monthly Installments specifies that the Maker (Borrower) is to pay the same amount each month for the period the money is owed.

Payment in Full by Date specifies that the Maker (Borrower) is to pay the entire amount at a future date.

Payment in Full on Demand specifies that no payment is due until the holder (Lender) sends a written notice (demand) for payment.

No. Install   **Enter the total number of monthly installments on this interest free note.**

[Example: 12, 24, 36, etc.]

Comment: Installments are periodic payments of equal amounts. Do not use '0'. The language of the note makes the balance of the principal due on the date of the last payment.

Install Amt2   **Enter the amount of each installment.**

[Example: 135.00]

Note: The program automatically adds commas where necessary. Use the right arrow key or decimal point to add cents.

Comment: Enter the figure in numbers. This amount is due the first day of each month. The language of the note makes the balance of the principal due on the date of the last payment.

Start Date2   **Enter the date of the first installment.**

[Example: 09/28/91]

Comment: This is the date that the first installment (payment) is due. Thereafter, the installment amount is due the first day of each month.

End Date2   **Enter the date of the last installment.**

[Example: 09/28/1991]

Comment: This is the date that the last installment (payment) is due.

Principal Due   **Enter the date on or by which the principal amount is to be paid to the holder of the note.**

[Example: 09/28/1991]

Comment: This is the date that the principal amount is due.

Prncpl Int Due   **Enter the date on or by which the principal amount plus interest is to be paid to the holder of the note.**

[Example: 09/28/1991]

Comment: This is the date that the principal amount and any accrued interest is due.

Note State   **Enter the state in which this note has been made.**

Comment: Use the two letter postal abbreviation for the state.

Sample Document[1]

PROMISSORY NOTE

FOR VALUE RECEIVED, the undersigned, Janet B. Williams, as maker, promises to pay to the order of Kenneth C. Parker, or any subsequent holder of this Note, the sum of five thousand dollars ($5,000.00) with interest from the date hereof at the rate of 12.00% per annum, calculated monthly, the principal and interest to be paid as set forth below.

Payment in Installments. Payment of principal and interest is to be made in twenty-four (24) equal monthly installments of two hundred thirty-five dollars and thirty-seven cents ($235.37). The first installment is due on January 1st, 1992, and subsequent installments are due on the first day of each month thereafter.

No Prepayment Penalty. The entire principal balance of this Note can be prepaid at any time without penalty.

Default - Waiver - Acceleration. In the event of default on this Note, Maker, Janet B. Williams, waives demand, presentment of payment, protest, notice of protest, dishonor and any defense by reason of any extension of time or other indulgence granted by the holder of this Note, and agrees that, if any payment on this Note is not made when due, the holder shall have the right to accelerate and make the entire unpaid balance of principal and interest immediately due and payable. Default is defined as:

a.   Failure to make any payment of principal or interest when due under the terms of this Note;

b.   The violation of any other term, condition or promise of this Note; or

c.   A filing by or against Maker, Janet B. Williams, of any Bankruptcy proceeding, or any filing of relief of debtors in any court or under any statute.

Costs. If the holder of this Note incurs any costs in the collection or enforcement of this Note, including costs of filing suit and reasonable attorney fees, Maker agrees to pay such costs.

Construction. If more than one party is named as the Maker of this Note, the obligations incurred by each party are joint and several.

---

[1] The sample document has been prepared and formatted for illustration purposes only. The actual document will print using the standard type style of your printer and the number of lines per page may differ.

This Note shall be interpreted in accordance with the laws of Ohio. No provision of this Note shall be affected by the invalidity of any other provision or provisions contained herein.

_____   _____
Janet B. Williams   Date

_____   _____
Witness   Date

Schedule of Payments

Date	Payment	Principal	Interest	Balance
2/01/92	$235.37	$185.37	$50.00	$4,814.63
3/01/92	$235.37	$187.23	$48.14	$4,627.40
4/01/92	$235.37	$189.10	$46.27	$4,438.30
5/01/92	$235.37	$190.99	$44.38	$4,247.31
6/01/92	$235.37	$192.90	$42.47	$4,054.41
7/01/92	$235.37	$194.83	$40.54	$3,859.58
8/01/92	$235.37	$196.78	$38.59	$3,662.80
9/01/92	$235.37	$198.75	$36.62	$3,464.05
10/01/92	$235.37	$200.73	$34.64	$3,263.32
11/01/92	$235.37	$202.74	$32.63	$3,060.58
12/01/92	$235.37	$204.77	$30.60	$2,855.81
1/01/93	$235.37	$206.82	$28.55	$2,648.99
2/01/93	$235.37	$208.89	$26.48	$2,440.10
3/01/93	$235.37	$210.97	$24.40	$2,229.13
4/01/93	$235.37	$213.08	$22.29	$2,016.05
5/01/93	$235.37	$215.21	$20.16	$1,800.84
6/01/93	$235.37	$217.37	$18.00	$1,583.47
7/01/93	$235.37	$219.54	$15.83	$1,363.93
8/01/93	$235.37	$221.74	$13.63	$1,142.19
9/01/93	$235.37	$223.95	$11.42	$918.24
10/01/93	$235.37	$226.19	$9.18	$692.05
11/01/93	$235.37	$228.45	$6.92	$463.60
12/01/93	$235.37	$230.74	$4.63	$232.86
1/01/94	$235.18	$232.86	$2.32	$.00

Demand for Money Owed

Document Summary

The Demand Letter for Money Owed should be used as a final request for payment of a legitimate debt owed to you. It allows the debtor to make payment in thirty days or face additional collection measures. If the debt remains unpaid after the expiration of the thirty-day period, you may wish to pursue a variety of collection options, including turning the debt over to a collection agency, filing a lawsuit, or beginning an action in small claims court. Because the laws vary from state to state, we suggest you consult with an attorney regarding the options available in your state. Your state or local bar association can provide a referral to an attorney who can help you.

If someone has written an NSF check, you may want to first notify that person using the Bad Check Notice.

Keep in mind that this letter is intended for the collection of personal debts ONLY, and should not be used in a commercial setting, or to collect money owed to someone else. Federal and state laws strictly regulate commercial collection practices.

Questions and Comments

Note: The following describes every question for the Demand for Money Owed. However, during the Question and Answer session, the program will display only those questions relevant to your personal situation.

Legal Name   **Please enter your full legal name.**

[Example: Jonathan A. Doe]

Comment: Do not use any nicknames or abbreviations. The name must be the legal name, not the social name. For example, the proper way to name John Smith's wife is Barbara S. Smith; it is not correct to use Mrs. John Smith.

Creditor Addr   **Enter your street address.**

[Example: 1270 Anystreet, Suite 135]

Comment: If the street address is more than one line, use commas to separate each part.

City State Zip   **Enter your city, state and zip code.**

[Example: Jacksonville, MS 98139]

Comment: Use the name of the community as named by the United States Post Office. Do not use the name of a real estate subdivision unless it is used as a Post Office address.

Enter the city, state, zip code. Use the two-letter state abbreviation, and use at least the five digit zip code. The state abbreviations are listed under the *Help Topics.*

Letter Date   **Enter the date you intend to send this letter.**

[Example: 09/28/91]

Comment: Use the MM/DD/YY format. It is not necessary to spell out the date.

Debtor Sal   **Enter the courtesy title of your debtor for use in the salutation.**

[Example: Mr., Mrs., Ms., or Dr.]

Comment: See the examples provided as a guide.

Debtor First   **Enter the first name of your debtor.**

[Example: Mary]

Comment: Do not use any abbreviations or nicknames.

Middle Init   **Enter the middle initial (optional).**

[Example: B.]

Comment: Use of the initial is optional. Include the period after the initial.

Debtor Last   **Enter the last name of your debtor.**

[Example: Smith]

Comment: Do not use any abbreviations or nicknames.

Debtor Addr   **Enter the street address of your debtor.**

[Example: 1270 Anystreet, Suite 135]

Comment: If the street address is more than one line, use commas to separate each part.

Debtor CSZ   **Enter the city, state and zip code of your debtor.**

[Example: Seattle, WA 98139]

Comment: Use the name of the community as named by the United States Post Office. Do not use the name of a real estate sub-division unless it is used as a Post Office address.

Enter the city, state, zip code. Use the two-letter state abbreviation, and use at least the five digit zip code. The state abbreviations are listed under the *Help Topics*.

Demand Amount   **Enter the amount you are demanding in this letter.**

[Example: 1,350.00]

Note: The program automatically adds commas where necessary.

Comment: Enter the full amount in dollars and cents. Use the right arrow key or decimal point to add cents.

Total Owed   **Is the amount you are demanding in this letter the total amount owed you?**

( ) YES
( ) NO

Comment: Select "NO" if you are demanding only partial payment of the total amount owed. Otherwise, select "YES".

Total Amount **Enter the total amount you are owed.**

[Example: 730.00]

Note: The program automatically adds commas where necessary.

Comment: Enter the full amount in dollars and cents. Use the right arrow key or decimal point to add cents.

Act Note Agmt **On what do you base your demand for payment?**

( ) Note
( ) Agreement
( ) Personal Loan
( ) Account No.
( ) Other

Comment: Select your choice.

If you select account, the next question will asked you to enter the account number. If your demand is based upon a written note or agreement, this letter requires you to include a copy of that written note or agreement.

Acct Number **Enter your Account Number.**

[Example: 000 159 456 7890]

Comment: Enter the account number carefully and check it again for accuracy.

Explain Debt **Using full sentences explain the basis for the debt.**

[Example: You owe me for the money I gave you to buy the Mexican blanket on our trip. I did not get the blanket or the money back.]

Comment: Select <NEXT> to move to the next question.

Days To Pay   **How many days does debtor have to make full payment?**

[Example: 30]

Comment: Thirty (30) days is commonly the number of days allowed before additional steps are taken.

No Pay Action   **Do you want to specify action taken if payment is not made?**

( ) YES
( ) NO

Comment: Select "Yes" if you want to describe the actions you intend to take if payment is not made within the specified time. Otherwise, select "No".

Action No Pay   **Describe the action you intend to take if payment is not received.**

[Example: the balance of the material originally ordered will not be delivered.]

Comment: Use complete sentences. Do not start the sentence with a capital letter. Be sure to follow the last sentence with a period (.).

Letterhead   **Will you be printing this letter on letterhead?**

( ) YES
( ) NO

Comment: Selecting "NO" will cause the program to print your return address at the top of the document. Selecting "YES" will add blank lines to accommodate letterhead paper.

Sample Document[1]

2309 Elm St.
Jacksonville, MS 78123

October 1, 1991

Mr. James D. Jackson
1209 Oak St.
Seattle, WA 98139

RE: Demand For Money Owed

Dear Mr. Jackson:

This letter will serve as a final demand for payment in the amount of one thousand, three hundred fifty dollars ($1,350.00) on our Note, a copy of which is enclosed.

Unless full payment of this amount is made within 30 days, I will take all steps necessary to enforce my legal rights and remedies in this matter.

Your prompt attention to this matter is anticipated and expected.

Sincerely,

Jonathan G. Smith

Enclosure: Note

---

[1] The sample document has been prepared and formatted for illustration purposes only. The actual document will print using the standard type style of your printer and the number of lines per page may differ.

Bad Check Notice

Document Summary

The Bad Check Notice should be used when a check you have received is returned by the bank for insufficient funds. It notifies the person who gave you the check that the check has been returned and that you will expect payment in cash or with a money order. As with the Demand Letter for Money Owed, this letter is intended for use in a non-commercial situation. You should not use this letter to collect on a check made to your business, or to collect for a check made to someone else. Federal and state laws strictly regulate commercial collection practices.

Questions and Comments

Note: The following describes <u>every</u> question for the Bad Check Notice. However, during the Question and Answer session, the program will display only those questions relevant to your personal situation.

Legal Name

Please enter your full legal name.

[Example: Jonathan A. Doe]

Comment: Do not use any nicknames or abbreviations. The name must be the legal name, not the social name.

Creditor Addr

Enter your street address.

[Example: 1270 Anystreet, Suite 135]

Comment: If the street address is more than one line, use commas to separate each part.

City State Zip

Enter your city, state and zip code.

[Example: Jacksonville, MS 98139]

Comment: Use the name of the community as named by the United States Post Office. Do not use the name of a real estate subdivision unless it is used as a Post Office address.

Enter the city, state, zip code. Use the two-letter state abbreviation, and use at least the five digit zip code. The state abbreviations are listed under the Help Topics.

Letter Date   **Enter the date you intend to send this letter.**

[Example: 09/28/91]

Comment: Use the MM/DD/YY format. It is not necessary to spell out the date.

Debtor Sal   **Enter the courtesy title of your debtor for use in the salutation.**

[Example: Mr., Mrs., Ms., or Dr.]

Comment: See the examples provided as a guide.

Debtor First   **Enter the first name of your debtor.**

[Example: Mary]

Comment: Do not use any abbreviations or nicknames.

Middle Init   **Enter the middle initial (optional).**

[Example: B.]

Comment: Use of the initial is optional. Include the period after the initial.

Debtor Last   **Enter the last name of your debtor.**

[Example: Smith]

Comment: Do not use any abbreviations or nicknames.

Debtor Addr   **Enter the street address of your debtor.**

[Example: 1270 Anystreet, Suite 135]

Comment: If the street address is more than one line, use commas to separate each part.

Debtor CSZ   **Enter the city, state and zip code of your debtor.**

[Example: Seattle, WA 98139]

Comment: Use the name of the community as named by the United States Post Office. Do not use the name of a real estate sub-division unless it is used as a Post Office address.

Enter the city, state, zip code. Use the two-letter state abbreviation, and use at least the five digit zip code. The state abbreviations are listed under the Help Topics.

Check Date   **Enter the date of the check.**

[Example: 09/28/91]

Comment: Use the MM/DD/YY format. It is not necessary to spell out the date.

Check Amount   **Enter the amount for which the check is written.**

[Example: 1,350.00]

Note: The program automatically adds commas where necessary.

Comment: Enter the full amount in dollars and cents. Use the right arrow key or decimal point to add cents.

Bad Check Act   **Are you taking or withholding some action as a result of the bad check?**

( ) YES
( ) NO

Comment: Select "No" if no action will be taken. Select "Yes" to explain what you intend to do (i.e. withhold service).

Action Bad Check

In a complete sentence, describe any action you are taking or withholding as a result of the returned check.

[Example: I will be unable to send you the quilt you requested until I receive this payment.]

Comment: If the returned check was written as payment for some service or product, your letter should include a statement of how the returned check is delaying receipt of the product or service.

Letterhead

Will you be printing this letter on letterhead?

( ) YES
( ) NO

Comment: Selecting "NO" will cause the program to print your return address at the top of the document. Selecting "YES" will add blank lines to accommodate letterhead paper.

Sample Document[1]

3495 Hillcrest Drive
Cleveland, OH 44115

October 1, 1991

Mr. James T. Clark
9954 Valley View Drive
Garfield Hts, OH 44176

RE: Your Check

Dear Mr. Clark:

Your check dated September 15th, 1991 in the amount of five hundred dollars ($500.00) has been returned by your bank for insufficient funds.

Please arrange to immediately replace this check with cash or money order. When you make the replacement payment, your old check will be returned to you.

Thank you for your anticipated cooperation in this matter.

Sincerely,

Jonathan H. Williams

---

[1] The sample document has been prepared and formatted for illustration purposes only. The actual document will print using the standard type style of your printer and the number of lines per page may differ.

Request for Credit Report

Document Summary

The Request for Credit Report directs a local credit bureau to provide you with a copy of the information contained in your records at the bureau. A number of studies show that many credit bureau records contain inaccurate information. You should request a credit report periodically to review the information it contains and correct any inaccurate or incomplete information. You may also want to review your credit record before you apply for credit, as inaccurate information could result in a credit refusal.

Most credit bureaus charge a fee of $5 or $10 for providing a report. However, if you have been refused credit in the last thirty days, you may obtain a copy of the report free of charge. The company that refuses to extend credit to you must tell you the name of the credit bureau it used in making its decision.

Questions and Comments

Note: The following describes every question for the Request for Credit Report. However, during the Question and Answer session, the program will display only those questions relevant to your personal situation.

User Name   **Enter your full legal name.**

[Example: Jonathan A. Doe]

Comment: Do not use any nicknames or abbreviations. Your name must be the legal name, not the social name.

User Address   **Enter your street address.**

[Example: 1270 Anystreet, Suite 135]

Comment: When the mailing address is more than one line, use commas to separate each part.

User CSZ **Enter your city, state and zip code.**

[Example: Seattle, WA 98139]

Comment: Use the name of the community as named by the United States Post Office. Do not use the name of a real estate subdivision unless it is used as a Post Office address.

Letter Date **Enter the date you intend to send this letter.**

[Example: 09/28/91]

Comment: Use the MM/DD/YY format. It is not necessary to spell out the date.

Credit Bureau **Enter the name of the local credit bureau to which you are mailing your request.**

[Example: ABC Credit Company]

Comment: Use the full name of the credit bureau you select. There may be several credit bureaus or agencies in your community.

Prior to preparing this written request for a credit report, you should check the telephone directory in your area for the name and address of a credit bureau or agency in your area. Call the credit bureau to identify the fee to be paid for your credit report copy. If you have been denied credit in the last 30 days, there should be no charge.

Bureau Add **Enter the street address of the local credit bureau to which you are mailing your request.**

[Example: 1270 Anystreet, Suite 135]

If the street address is more than one line, use commas to separate each part.

Cr Bureau CSZ **Enter the city, state and zip code of the local credit bureau to which you are mailing your request.**

[Example: Seattle, WA 98139]

Comment: Use the name of the community as named by the United States Post Office. Do not use the name of a real estate subdivision unless it is used as a Post Office address.

Current Addr	**Have you lived at your current address for three or more years?** *( ) YES* *( ) NO* **Comment:** The credit bureau uses your name and your address to find your records.
Prev Address	**Enter your previous street address.** *[Example: 1270 Anystreet, Suite 135]* **Comment:** Because you have lived at your current address less than three years, the credit bureau requires that you provide your previous address when requesting a credit report.
Prev Add CSZ	**Enter the city, state and zip code of your previous address.** *[Example: Seattle, WA 98139]* **Comment:** Because you have lived at your current address less than three years, the credit bureau requires that you provide your previous address when requesting a credit report.
User Employer	**Enter the name of your employer.** *[Example: XYZ Manufacturing]* **Comment:** If you are not employed at this time, enter "Not Currently Employed".
User DOB	**Enter your date of birth.** *[Example: 08/25/1956]* **Comment:** Use the MM/DD/YY format. It is not necessary to spell out the date.

SSN User **Enter your Social Security Number.**

[Example: 159-45-6789]

Comment: Double-check the number to make sure you have entered it correctly. It is very important to record the number accurately.

Married **Are you married?**

( ) YES
( ) NO

Comment: If you are married, this program assumes that you want to obtain a joint (rather than an individual) credit report. If you want your own credit report, even though you are married, answer "No".

Spouse Name **Please enter your spouse's full legal name.**

[Example: Mary B. Doe]

Comment: Enter your spouse's full legal name, first name first, last name last. Please do not use nicknames or your spouse's social name. For example, use "Mary B. Doe" not "Mrs. John Doe."

Spouse Emplr **Enter the name of your spouse's employer.**

[Example: Harris Publishing]

Comment: If your spouse is not employed at this time, enter "Not Currently Employed".

Spouse DOB **Enter your spouse's date of birth.**

[Example: 11/16/1958]

Comment: Use the MM/DD/YY format. It is not necessary to spell out the date.

SSN Spouse
: **Enter your spouse's Social Security Number.**

[Example: 987-65-4321]

Comment: Double-check the number to make sure you have entered it correctly. It is very important to record the number accurately.

Denied Credit
: **Have you been denied credit within the last 30 days?**

( ) YES
( ) NO

Comment: If you have been denied credit within the last 30 days, your credit report should be provided free of charge. Otherwise, there is a small fee to obtain your credit report.

Who Deny
: **Enter the name of the company, agency or organization which denied you credit within the last 30 days.**

[Example: J. C. Penney]

Comment: Be sure to enter the full name of the company. Your credit report may also include the names of all persons or organizations who have seen your credit report over the last 6 months.

How Pay Fee
: **How are you paying the fee to obtain your credit report?**

( ) Check
( ) Money Order

Comment: The fee for your credit report must be enclosed with this letter. Payment must be made by check or money order payable to the credit bureau. The fee must accompany the letter.

Report Fee
: **Enter the amount of the fee to be paid for your credit report.**

[Example: 25.00]

Comment: Enter the Report Fee amount in dollars and cents. Use the right arrow key or decimal point to add cents.

Phone Business **Enter a telephone number at which you can be contacted during business hours.**

[Example: 242-555-1270]

Comment: Be sure to include your area code. Check the number for accuracy.

You should receive your credit report copy within a week. Upon receipt, carefully review the information provided in the report. You have a right to respond to a negative entry on your report and to have your response made part of your credit report.

Letterhead **Will you be printing this letter on letterhead?**

( ) YES
( ) NO

Comment: Selecting "NO" will cause the program to print your return address at the top of the document. Selecting "YES" will add blank lines to accommodate letterhead paper.

Sample Document[1]

2394 Oak St.
Seattle, WA 98139

October 1, 1991

ABC Credit Company
4590 Lake Ave., Suite 650
Seattle, WA 98139

RE: Credit Report

Dear Sir or Madam:

Please consider this letter my request for a copy of my credit report. I provide the
following information to expedite this request:

My Full Name:	Jonathan A. Jones
My Spouse's Name:	Mary B. Jones
My Current Address:	2394 Oak St.
	Seattle, WA 98139
My Employer:	XYZ Manufacturing
My Spouse's Employer:	Harris Publishing
My Birth Date:	09/25/1956
My Spouse's Birth Date:	11/16/1958
My Social Security #:	349-83-4953
My Spouse's Soc. Sec. #:	505-95-3838

Within the last thirty days, J.C. Penney denied us credit. We are therefore requesting that
our credit report be provided free of charge.

If there are any questions, please call (206) 555-4949 during regular business hours to
speak with one of us.

Thank you in advance for your assistance in this matter.

Sincerely,

Jonathan A. Jones

Mary B. Jones

---

[1] The sample document has been prepared and formatted for illustration purposes only. The
actual document will print using the standard type style of your printer and the number of lines
per page may differ.

Request for Credit Report Correction

Document Summary

This letter notifies a credit bureau of an error contained in the bureau's records. Under the federal Fair Credit Reporting Act, credit bureaus are required to investigate and correct inaccurate information.

During the investigation, the bureau must indicate to anyone requesting a report that the alleged inaccuracy is being challenged. If the investigation determines that the information is erroneous, the credit bureau is required to correct the report. Even if the negative information is correct, the law allows you to enter an explanatory statement in your credit record, and this statement must be included in any reports issued by the bureau.

If you discover an error in your credit record at one bureau, there's a better than average chance that the error is in another bureau's files. We suggest you use the Request for Credit Report letter contained in this program to contact the major credit bureaus in your area. The nation's three largest credit bureaus are TRW, TransUnion, and Equifax. You can find their addresses in your local telephone directory.

Questions and Comments

Note: The following describes every question for the Request for Credit Correction. However, during the Question and Answer session, the program will only display those questions relevant to your personal situation.

User Name   Enter the full legal name of the person requesting the report.

[Example: Jonathan A. Doe]

Comment: Do not use any nicknames or abbreviations. The name must be the legal name, not the social name.

User Address   **Enter your street address.**

[Example: 1270 Anystreet, Suite 135]

Comment: When the mailing address is more than one line, use commas to separate each part.

CSZ   **Enter your city, state and zip code.**

[Example: Seattle, WA 98139]

Comment: Use the name of the community as named by the United States Post Office. Do not use the name of a real estate subdivision unless it is used as a Post Office address.

Letter Date   **Enter the date you intend to send this letter.**

[Example: 09/28/91]

Comment: Use the MM/DD/YY format. It is not necessary to spell out the date.

Credit Bureau   **Enter the name of the local credit bureau to which you are mailing your request.**

[Example: ABC Credit Company]

Comment: Use the full name of the credit bureau you select. There may be several credit bureaus or agencies in your community.

Press [F1] for additional comments.

Prior to preparing this written request for a credit report, you should check the telephone directory in your area for the name and address of a credit bureau or agency in your area. Call the credit bureau to identify the fee to be paid for your credit report copy. If you have been denied credit in the last 30 days, there should be no charge.

Cr Bureau Add   **Enter the street address of the local credit bureau to which you are mailing your request.**

[Example: 1270 Anystreet, Suite 135]

Comment: If the street address is more than one line, use commas to separate each part.

Cr Bureau CSZ

Enter the city, state and zip code of the local credit bureau to which you are mailing your request.

[Example: Seattle, WA 98139]

Comment: Use the name of the community as named by the United States Post Office. Do not use the name of a real estate subdivision unless it is used as a Post Office address.

Describe Error

Enter a description of the error contained in your credit bureau report.

[Example: Account # 13544 at Henderson's House of Hardware is listed as an open account that is 90 days past due. This account was closed July 1, 1989, and was paid in full at that time.

Comment: You may enter a statement of up to 12 lines here. You may also want to enclose a photocopy of the credit report with the erroneous information highlighted.

LetterHead

Will you be printing this letter on letterhead?

( ) YES
( ) NO

Comment: Selecting "No" will cause the program to print your return address at the top of the document. Selecting "Yes" will add blank lines to accommodate letterhead paper.

Sample Document[1]

1270 Anystreet, Suite 135
Seattle, WA 98139

October 1st, 1991

ABC Credit Company
1234 E. 9th St., Suite 200
Seattle, WA 98139

RE: Credit Report Error

Dear Sir or Madam:

A review of my credit report indicates that it contains information which is incorrect. As provided for under the federal Fair Credit Reporting Act, I hereby request that you correct the following information:

Account # 13544 at Anderson's Hardware Store is listed as on open account that is 90 days past due. This account was closed July 1, 1989, and was paid in full at that time.

I also request that this letter be made a part of my file and included with any report issued by you in response to a request for credit information about me.

Thank you for your prompt attention to this matter.

Sincerely,

Jonathan A. Doe

---

[1] The sample document has been prepared and formatted for illustration purposes only. The actual document will print using the standard type style of your printer and the number of lines per page may differ.

Motor Vehicle Bill of Sale

Document Summary

Home Lawyer's Bill of Sale for Motor Vehicle is used to transfer ownership of a motor vehicle from one person to another person. A motor vehicle can be an automobile, truck, motorcycle, motor home, boat or trailer. If the seller has a title issued by the state which describes the item as a motor vehicle, use this form to transfer ownership.

Many of the cases that go to court over used cars involve problems that arise weeks or months after the buyer has owned the car. The buyer may discover defects with the car's mechanical systems (engine, brakes, air conditioning, etc.) or problems with its physical condition (rusting body panels, worn muffler or exhaust system). In either situation, the seller is best protected when a bill of sale is prepared clearly stating that the automobile is sold in an "as is" condition. This means that the buyer accepts the vehicle with no warranty from the seller about the condition of the vehicle.

The Bill of Sale should only be given to the buyer upon receipt of payment in full. Giving the Bill of Sale before receiving full payment can lead to problems in the future.

The Bill of Sale helps the buyer obtain insurance for the vehicle. It also helps prove ownership in the event the buyer decides to resell the vehicle later on.

The Bill of Sale for Motor Vehicle also contains an odometer statement. At the time of sale, check the appropriate box regarding vehicle mileage.

The Bill of Sale for Motor Vehicle should be signed in the presence of a notary public. A number of states also require that the certificate of title for the motor vehicle be signed and notarized as well. You can contact your county law librarian or an attorney for information about the law in your state. Free or low cost notary service is available at many banks and financial institutions. Check with your bank to see if a notary is available.

Questions and Comments

Note: The following describes <u>every</u> question for the Motor Vehicle Bill of Sale. However, during the Question and Answer session, the program will display only those questions relevant to your personal situation.

Seller   **Is there more than one seller?**

( ) YES
( ) NO

Comment: This program allows up to two sellers. Answer "YES" if the certificate of title shows the name of two owners. Answer "NO" if the title shows the name of only one.

Seller   **Enter the full legal name of the seller.**

[Example: Susan B. Doe]

Comment: Enter the seller's name (the owner) exactly as it appears on the certificate of title for the motor vehicle being sold.

Seller 2   **Enter the full legal name of the second seller.**

[Example: Jonathan A. Doe]

Comment: Enter the seller's name (the owner) exactly as it appears on the certificate of title for the motor vehicle being sold.

Sale Price Car   **Enter the sale price of the motor vehicle described in this Bill of Sale.**

[Example: 5,000.00]

Note: The program automatically adds commas where necessary.

Comment: Enter the sale price of the car in dollars and cents. Use the right arrow key or decimal point to add cents.

Buyer   **Is there more than one buyer?**

( ) YES
( ) NO

Comment: The program allows you to enter up to two buyers.

Buyer 1   **Enter the full legal name of the first buyer.**

[Example: Mary A. Smith]

Comment: Do not use any nicknames or abbreviations.

Buyer 2   **Enter the full legal name of the second buyer.**

[Example: William C. Smith]

Comment: Do not use any nicknames or abbreviations.

Buyer Address   **Enter the street address of the buyer.**

[Example: 1270 Anystreet, Suite 135]

Comment: If the street address is more than one line, use commas to separate each part.

Buyer City   **Enter the city of the buyer.**

[Example: Cleveland]

Comment: It is not necessary to follow the city with a comma. Use the name of the community as named by the United States Post Office.

Buyer State   **Enter the state of the buyer.**

[Example: OH]

Comment: Use the two-letter state abbreviation.

Buyer Zip   **Enter the zip code of the buyer.**

[Example: 98136-1351]

Comment: Use the nine-digit zip code when possible. The five-digit zip code is required on most documents and for most mailing addresses. The nine-digit zip code helps speed mail delivery.

Sell Address   **Enter the street address of the seller.**

[Example: 1270 Anystreet, Suite 135]

Comment: If the street address is more than one line, use commas to separate each part.

Sell City   **Enter the city of the seller.**

[Example: Cleveland]

Comment: It is not necessary to follow the city with a comma. Use the name of the community as named by the United States Post Office.

Sell State   **Enter the state of the seller.**

[Example: OH]

Comment: Use the two-letter abbreviation for the state.

Sell Zip   **Enter the zip code of the seller.**

[Example: 91236-1351]

Comment: Use the nine-digit zip code when possible. The nine-digit zip code helps speed mail delivery. The five-digit zip code is required on most documents and for most mailing addresses.

Year   **Enter the year of the vehicle being sold.**

[Example: 1989]

Comment: Be sure to use all four numbers. Do not abbreviate the year to the last two digits: 1989 not 89.

Make   **Enter the make of the vehicle being sold.**

[Example: Chevrolet]

Comment: This blank is for the make of the vehicle only.

Model   **Enter the model of the vehicle being sold.**

[Example: Blazer]

Comment: This blank is for the model of the vehicle only.

Body Style   **Enter the style of the vehicle being sold.**

[Example: 2-door, 4x4]

Comment: Make the style completely descriptive. For example: 4-door station wagon.

Color   **Enter a description of the vehicle being sold.**

[Example: Red]

Comment: The description includes the color and other special features. When the vehicle has more than one color, include both. List the predominant color first.

Serial Number   **Enter the serial or vehicle identification number of the vehicle being sold.**

[Example: 1A2BC34D5EF678900]

Comment: Enter the serial or vehicle identification number (VIN) exactly as it appears on the certificate of title and the vehicle being sold.

Sample Document[1]

BILL OF SALE OF
MOTOR VEHICLE

In consideration of ten thousand dollars ($10,000.00), paid to me this day by Fredrick J. Jones, as buyer, whose address is 123 Main Street, Columbus, Ohio 43210-0123, I, Thomas F. Watson, whose address is 55 Cedar Rd., Columbus, Ohio 43215-0101, hereby grant, transfer, sell and deliver to buyer the following motor vehicle:

1990 Chevrolet Blazer
2-door 4x4
COLOR: Black
VIN: 23WEDF9348DSK

I warrant that I have good title to the motor vehicle referred to above, that there are no liens or encumbrances other than those shown on the certificate of title, and that I have the right to sell the motor vehicle. I agree to discharge any and all liens and encumbrances shown on the certificate of title, and I will defend the buyer against any claims made against the motor vehicle.

This motor vehicle is sold "as is" and "where is." No warranties, either express or implied, as to the condition of the motor vehicle are made.

Check One

_____ Seller represent that the odometer reading on this motor vehicle is _____ miles and that, to the best of his or her knowledge, corresponds to the actual mileage of the vehicle.

_____ Seller represent that, to the best of his or her knowledge, the odometer reading on this vehicle exceeds 135,000 miles.

_____ Seller represent that, to the best of his or her knowledge, the odometer reading for this motor vehicle is inaccurate.

I hereby certify under penalty of perjury that the statements made above are true and correct to the best of my knowledge.

---

[1] The sample document has been prepared and formatted for illustration purposes only. The actual document will print using the standard type style of your printer and the number of lines per page may differ.

Date   Thomas F. Watson

Sworn to and subscribed before me this _____ day of _____,
19___.

My Commission Expires:

_____   NOTARY PUBLIC

(SEAL)

General Bill of Sale

Document Summary

Home Lawyer's General Bill of Sale allows one person to transfer ownership of an item of personal property to another. Personal property is anything a person owns other than real estate.

The seller should only give a General Bill of Sale to the buyer upon receipt of payment in full from the buyer.

Obviously, you won't need to provide a Bill of Sale for every item of personal property. You should use the General Bill of Sale, however, for larger items, such as stereo or video equipment, and expensive items, such as jewelry and antiques.

The General Bill of Sale protects the seller from future claims of misrepresentation regarding the item sold. Home Lawyer's General Bill of Sale notes that the item described is sold "as is. "This means that the buyer accepts the item from the seller with no warranty as to the condition of the item.

A Bill of Sale is also helpful for the buyer's use in obtaining insurance on expensive items. It also helps prove ownership of the item in the event the buyer decides to resell the item later on.

Some states require a notarized Bill of Sale for certain items, such as firearms. You can contact your county law librarian or an attorney for information about the law in your state. Home Lawyer's General Bill of Sale includes a notary statement. Even if it's not required, it won't hurt to use a notary statement for any item you sell. Free or low cost notary service is available at many banks or other financial institutions. Check with your bank to see if a notary is available.

Questions and Comments

Note: The following describes <u>every</u> question for the General Bill of Sale. However, during the Question and Answer session, the program will display only those questions relevant to your personal situation.

Sale Price Prp   **What is the price for which the item covered by this Bill of Sale is being sold?**

[Example: 13,500.00]

Note: The program automatically adds commas where necessary.

Comment: Enter the full amount (dollars and cents) of the sale price. Use the right arrow key or decimal point to add cents.

Buyer Name   **Enter the full legal name of the buyer.**

[Example: Jonathan A. Doe]

Comment: Do not use any nicknames or abbreviations. The name must be the legal name, not the social name.

Buyer Address   **Enter the street address of the buyer.**

[Example: 1270 Anystreet, Suite 135]

Comment: If the street address is more than one line, use commas to separate each part.

Buyer City   **Enter the city of the buyer.**

[Example: Cleveland]

Comment: It is not necessary to follow the city with a comma. Use the name of the community as named by the United States Post Office.

Buyer State   **Enter the state of the buyer.**

[Example: OH]

Comment: Use the two-letter state abbreviation.

Buyer Zip	**Enter the zip code of the buyer.**

[Example: 98136-1351]

Comment: Use the nine-digit zip code when possible. The five-digit zip code is required on most documents and for most mailing addresses. The nine-digit zip code helps speed mail delivery. |
| **Seller Name** | **Enter the full legal name of the seller.**

[Example: Mary S. Smith]

Comment: Do not use any nicknames or abbreviations. The name must be the legal name, not the social name. |
| **Sell Address** | **Enter the street address of the seller.**

[Example: 1270 Anystreet, Suite 135]

Comment: If the street address is more than one line, use commas to separate each part. |
| **Sell City** | **Enter the city of the seller.**

[Example: Cleveland]

Comment: It is not necessary to follow the city with a comma. Use the name of the community as named by the United States Post Office. |
| **Sell State** | **Enter the state of the seller.**

[Example: OH]

Comment: Use the two-letter abbreviation for the state. |
| **Sell Zip** | **Enter the zip code of the seller.**

[Example: 91236-1351]

Comment: Use the nine-digit zip code when possible. The nine-digit zip code helps speed mail delivery. The five-digit zip code is required on most documents and for most mailing addresses. |

Sell Property   **Enter a description of the item being sold.**

Comment: Describe the item being sold as completely and accurately as possible. (Include manufacturer, type of property, model number, serial number, color, etc.).

For example: A 19 inch RCA color television with stereo, Model #RC-19, Serial #123456789. It is not necessary to include a period at the end of the description.

Sample Document[1]

GENERAL BILL OF SALE

In consideration of three thousand, five hundred dollars ($3,500.00), paid to me this day by Jonathon A. Smith, as buyer, whose address is 3409 Elm St., Cleveland, Ohio 44111, I, Mary S. Jackson, whose address is 3402 Reynolds Ave., Cleveland, Ohio 44112, hereby grant, transfer, sell and deliver to buyer the following property: A Hewlett Packard lap Top Computer, Model LS/12, serial no. 234ASD456, complete with a 40 MB hard disk drive and an internal modem.

I agree that I will warrant and defend the buyer, the buyer's personal representatives, successors and assigns against any claims made by any person against this property.

This property is sold "as is" and "where is," and no warranties express or implied are made as to the condition of this property.

_____   _____
Date   Mary S. Jackson

Sworn to and subscribed before me this _____ day of _____,
19___.

My Commission Expires:
_____   _____
NOTARY PUBLIC

(SEAL)

---

[1] The sample document has been prepared and formatted for illustration purposes only. The actual document will print using the standard type style of your printer and the number of lines per page may differ.

**Residential
Lease**

Document Summary

The Residential Lease Agreement can be used if you are renting
part or all of your house, or if you own a duplex or an apartment
complex. Our clients often ask, "Do I need a lease?" Whether you
are the one renting an apartment or house (the Tenant) or own
rental property (the Landlord), a written lease is recommended.

As a Landlord you expect to receive the agreed upon amount of rent
by a specific date each month. If your money doesn't arrive as
promised, you might call or write the Tenant asking for your rental
payment. If your Tenant fails to respond and days pass, Landlords
have legal rights to recover the apartment and collect their money.
This may require an eviction action (going to court). The written
residential lease is very helpful in determining the rights of both
parties involved in a rental situation. Without the lease, the
Landlord and Tenant may dispute what was said and agreed to when
the apartment was first rented.

Home Lawyer's Residential Lease Agreement allows a Landlord to
rent a house or apartment to a Tenant for a specified period of time.
Most residential leases run for a period of six months or one year.
We recommend that you use this Agreement for leases no longer
than one year in duration.

Before signing this or any other residential lease agreement, both
the Landlord and Tenant should take several steps to minimize any
problems that could arise later on. The Landlord should be sure
that the property is in reasonably safe and sanitary condition. In
many communities, the law requires that any rental property be
equipped with deadbolt locks, smoke detectors and fire
extinguishers. You can obtain information about the requirements
in your locale by contacting your community housing authority or
codes enforcement agency.

If the property is being rented for the first time, the Landlord should
also contact the insurance company that carries the policy on the
property to determine whether any changes in coverage will be
necessary.

Before signing the Residential Lease Agreement, the Landlord and Tenant should conduct an inspection of the premises, and note in writing any defects or damage, such as torn wallpaper, defective light switches or electrical outlets, broken windows, and so on. Both the Landlord and Tenant should sign and date the inspection report. Doing so will help to protect the Tenant from any later claim that the damage was caused by the Tenant.

The Tenant should also obtain insurance on his or her personal property, as the Landlord will not be responsible for any damage or loss the Tenant suffers.

The Landlord and Tenant should both receive a signed original of the Residential Lease Agreement.

Questions and Comments

Note: The following describes <u>every</u> question for the Residential Lease. However, during the Question and Answer session, the program will display only those questions relevant to your personal situation.

Landlord   **Enter the full legal name of the Landlord(s) of the premises to be leased. Home Lawyer will allow up to 2 landlords.**

[Example: *Jonathan A. Doe*
              Mary S. Smith]

Comment: Enter the names of up to two persons as Landlord, one name on each line. Press [Enter] to move to the next line. When you have finished, select <NEXT> to move to the next question.

Tenant   **Enter the full legal name of the Tenant(s).**

[Example: *Susan B. Johnson*
              Mark S. Johnson]

Comment: Enter the names of up to four persons as Tenants, one name on each line. Press [Enter] to move to the next line. When you have finished, select <NEXT> to move to the next question.

Property Addr   **Enter the street address of the property to be leased.**

[Example: 1270 Anystreet, Apartment A]

Comment: When the address exceeds one line, use commas to separate each part. Give the actual street address of the property, not the postal address if the address is a box number.

Prop City   **Enter the name of the city of the property to be leased.**

[Example: Chicago]

Comment: It is not necessary to follow the city with a comma. Use the name of the community as named by the United States Post Office.

Prop State   **Enter the state of the property to be leased.**

[Example: IL]

Comment: Use the two-letter abbreviation for the state.

Prop Zip   **Enter the zip code of the property to be leased.**

[Example: 60606-1270]

Comment: Use the nine-digit zip code when possible. The nine-digit zip code helps speed mail delivery. The five-digit zip code is required on most documents and for most mailing addresses.

Furnished   **Will the premises be rented furnished?**

( ) YES
( ) NO

Comment: Select "YES" for furnished or "NO" for unfurnished. Furnished apartments typically contain beds, tables, chairs, etc.

Furniture   **Please list the furnishings included with the apartment.**

[Example: 2 beds, couch, kitchen table, and dishwasher]

Comment: The Tenant will be held responsible for these furnishings.

Storage   **Do you want to include a description of additional storage available to the Tenant?**

( ) YES
( ) NO

Comment: Select "YES" if you want to provide for additional storage space such as a garage, shed or basement storage area. Otherwise, select "NO".

Storage Desc   **Please enter a description of the storage area.**

[Example: storage area 4C in the
basement of the premises.]

Comment: Enter a clear and concise description of the storage area.

Parking   **Do you want to describe the parking facilities available to the Tenant?**

( ) YES
( ) NO

Comment: Select "YES" if you want to describe a specific area where the Tenant will be allowed to park. Otherwise, select "NO".

Parking Desc   **Enter a description of the parking facilities.**

[Example: spaces 4D and 4E in the
East parking lot.]

Comment: Enter a clear and concise description of the parking facilities designated for the Tenant's use.

Start Date   **Enter the date on which the lease will begin.**

[Example: 09/28/91]

Comment: This will be the first date that the Tenant can take possession of the premises (move in).

Expire Lease   **Enter the date on which the lease will expire.**

[Example: 09/28/92]

Comment: Enter the date that the lease will end. We recommend that the term of this Residential Lease not exceed one year.

Auto Renewal   **Do you want to provide for the automatic renewal of this lease?**

( ) YES
( ) NO

Comment: An automatic renewal extends the lease for a specified period of time unless either party gives notice of their intention to terminate the lease.

Renewal Term   **Enter the renewal term of the lease.**

[Example: six months]

Comment: Enter the renewal term in words. We recommend that this term be no longer than one year.

Terminate Notice   **Enter the number of days' notice required to terminate the lease.**

[Example: 30]

Comment: Enter a number from 10 to 30.

Rent Amount   **Enter the monthly rent in numbers.**

[Example: 500.00]

Comment: This is the amount due per month for rent. Enter the value in dollars and cents. Use the right arrow key or decimal point to add cents.

Day Rent Due   **Enter the day of the month on which rent is due.**

[Example: first]

Comment: The rent should be due regularly on a day which is clearly named, for example, the first, second, fifteenth, etc.

Fee   **Do you want to charge the Tenant a penalty fee for late payments?**

( ) YES
( ) NO

Comment: This is the amount that the Tenant will pay when the base rent is past due beyond a date specified by the Landlord.

State laws may limit the amount of penalty payment a Landlord may charge. You can contact your county law library or an attorney for information regarding the law in your state.

Fee Days   **Enter the number of days rent is past due before a penalty fee will be charged.**

[Example: 5]

Comment: For example, if you specify five days and the rent is due on the first of the month, a penalty will be charged if payment is not received within five days or by the sixth of the month.

Fee Amt   **Enter the dollar amount of the penalty due if the Tenant fails to make payments on time.**

[Example: 25.00]

Comment: Enter this figure in dollars and cents. Use the right arrow key or decimal point to add cents.

Security   **Will the Tenant be required to pay a security deposit?**

( ) YES
( ) NO

Comment: Press [F1] Help for Additional Comments about Security Deposits.

A security deposit is a refundable deposit given by a Tenant to a Landlord to protect against unusual damages to the leased premises caused by the Tenants or occupants.

A security deposit is not considered a cleaning deposit, and in many states, it may not be used to offset unpaid rent. Laws regarding security deposits vary widely from state to state.

In a number of states, Landlords must keep security deposits in separate, interest bearing accounts, and they must pay the accrued interest to the Tenant on a periodic basis. Other laws limit the amount that may be charged as a security deposit, and require the Landlord and Tenant to conduct inspections before and after the Tenant takes possession of the leased premises.

Failure to comply with all the requirements specified may allow the Tenant to recover two or even three times the amount of the security deposit as damages in a court action. In many states, Landlords must return the unused portion of the security deposit to the Tenant within thirty days after the Tenant vacates the property. Landlords may also be required to provide the Tenant with an itemized list of deductions taken from the security deposit.

IF YOU ARE UNFAMILIAR WITH THE LAWS REGARDING SECURITY DEPOSITS IN YOUR STATE, WE STRONGLY RECOMMEND THAT YOU CONSULT WITH AN ATTORNEY.

Comment Lease   *A SPECIAL NOTE ABOUT SECURITY DEPOSITS*

Because the laws regarding security deposits vary so widely, and because of the potential cost to the Landlord for violating these laws, we strongly recommend that you consult with an attorney for advice about the laws in your state.

Comment: Comment Only.

Security Amt   **Enter the dollar amount of the security deposit.**

[Example: 250.00]

Comment: Enter this figure in dollars and cents. Use the right arrow key or decimal point to add cents.

Occupants	**Enter the names of the individuals who will live in the premises during the term of this lease.**

[Example: *Susan B. Johnson*
              Mark S. Johnson
              Jennifer A. Johnson]

Comment: Enter the names of up to six persons as occupants, one name on each line. Press [Enter] to move to the next line. When you have finished, select <NEXT> to move to the next question.

The occupants are not the same as the Tenants. Occupants are the people who live in the apartment. Tenants are the people responsible for paying the rent.

Pets Allowed	**Are pets permitted on the premises?**

( ) YES
( ) NO

Comment: Select "YES" if pets are permitted or "NO" if pets are not permitted.

Pets	**Enter a description of any pets permitted on the premises during the term of this lease.**

[Example: *dog, Poodle, Buddy; and*
              cat, Persian, Tiger]

Comment: Describe the pets you will allow on the premises by type (dog, cat, etc.), breed (Poodle, Siamese, etc.) and name (Rover, Fluffy, etc.).

Utilities	**Enter all the utilities Tenant will pay for during the term of the lease.**

[Example: phone, electricity]

Comment: Include all utilities or services that will be the Tenant's responsibility, such as water, electricity, oil, gas, trash removal, etc.

Landlord Addr   **Enter the street address at which the Landlord will receive rent payments and notices regarding this lease.**

[Example: 1270 Anystreet, Suite 135]

Comment: This is the address that the Tenant will use to notify the Landlord of intent to terminate the lease. When the street address is more than one line, use commas to separate each part.

Landlord CSZ   **Enter the city, state and zip code at which the Landlord will receive rent payments and notices regarding this lease.**

[Example: Chicago, IL 60606]

Comment: This is the address that Tenant will use to notify Landlord of intent to terminate the lease.

Use the name of the community as named by the United States Post Office. Do not use the name of a real estate sub-division unless it is used as a Post Office address. Use the two-letter state abbreviation, and use at least the five digit zip code. The state abbreviations are listed under *Help Topics*.

Tenant Addr   **Enter the street address at which the Tenant will receive notices regarding this lease.**

[Example: 1270 Anystreet, Suite 135]

Comment: This is the address that Landlord will use to notify Tenant of defaults or intent to terminate the lease. In most cases, this will be the address of the premises being leased.

Tenant CSZ   **Enter the city, state and zip code at which the Tenant will receive notices regarding this lease.**

[Example: Chicago, IL 60606]

Comment: This is the address that Landlord will use to notify Tenant of defaults or intent to terminate the lease. In most cases, this will be the address of the premises being leased.

Use the name of the community as named by the United States Post Office. Do not use the name of a real estate sub-division unless it is used as a Post Office address. Use the two-letter state abbreviation, and use at least the five digit zip code. The state abbreviations are listed under *Help Topics*.

Sample Document[1]

RESIDENTIAL LEASE

This Lease is made this ____ day of _____, 19 ___, by and between
William J. Jones ("Landlord"), and Mark S. Johnson ("Tenant"). As used in this Lease, the
singular includes the plural and the masculine includes the feminine at all times.

1. Premises to be Leased. Landlord agrees to lease to Tenant the premises known
as and located at the following address:

190 Oak St., Apt 4B
Cleveland, Ohio 44111

The premises are rented unfurnished.

2. Term of Lease. This Lease shall begin at 12:01 a.m. on September 1st, 1991 and
end at 12:01 a.m. on September 1st, 1992. During the term of the Lease, Tenant shall pay
seven hundred dollars ($700.00) per month as rent to the Landlord. Rent shall be due on
the first day of each month through the term of this Lease.

3. Security Deposit. No security deposit shall be required.

4. Subletting. Tenant promises not to assign or transfer this Lease or any interest in
this Lease, or sublet the premises or any part of the premises without the prior written
consent of the Landlord.

5. Liens and Encumbrances. Tenant promises not to allow any liens or
encumbrances to attach to the premises.

6. Occupancy. Tenant shall be entitled to use the premises for residential purposes
only. The premises shall be occupied by the following persons and no others: Mark S.
Johnson. No pets shall be permitted on the premises.

7. Maintenance. Tenant shall maintain the premises in a safe and sanitary
condition; dispose of all garbage, rubbish and waste in a clean, safe and legal manner, the
storage of garbage on the premises being strictly prohibited; keep all plumbing fixtures in
the premises clean, sanitary and in good working order; use and operate all electrical
fixtures and plumbing fixtures properly; comply with all obligations imposed upon Tenants
by applicable provisions of housing, building and health codes; refrain, and forbid any other
person from destroying, defacing, damaging or removing any part of the premises.

---

[1] The sample document has been prepared and formatted for illustration purposes only. The
actual document will print using the standard type style of your printer and the number of lines
per page may differ.

Tenant shall not make any alterations to the premises or change any locks on the premises without the prior written consent of Landlord. Tenant shall not do anything on the premises that will increase or make voidable Landlord's insurance on the premises.

8. Storage. Tenant shall be entitled to store items of personal property in Storage area 4B in the basement of Building 4. Tenant acknowledges that all personal property stored in the area described in this paragraph is stored at Tenant's own risk, and Tenant agrees to hold Landlord harmless for any loss or damage to such property.

9. Parking. Tenant shall be entitled to use of the following described area for motor vehicle parking: spaces 4A and 4B in the West parking lot. Tenant acknowledges that any and all vehicles parked in the area described in this paragraph are parked at the Tenant's own risk.

10. Utilities. Tenant shall be responsible for all deposits and payments for the following utilities: telephone, electric, gas, water.

11. Landlord Duties. Landlord shall comply with the requirements of all building, housing and health codes as they apply to Landlord. Landlord shall pay all real estate taxes and assessments as due, but reserves the right to contest any such tax assessment.

12. Premises As Is. Tenant acknowledges that he has inspected the premises prior to signing this Lease and accepts the premises in its present condition, except as noted on the attached list incorporated in this Lease by reference.

13. Termination. Either party may terminate this Lease by giving the other party no less than sixty (60) days' notice in writing prior to the termination date of this Lease. Unless such notice is given, this Lease shall be extended on a month-to-month basis on the same terms, except that Landlord may increase the rent on the premises with thirty (30) days' notice. Upon termination of this Lease, Tenant agrees to return the premises to the Landlord in good repair and in a clean and sanitary condition, except for ordinary wear and tear.

14. Liabilities. Tenant agrees to assume all liability and hold Landlord harmless from any and all injuries to persons or damage to property caused by Tenant or any other person on the premises with Tenant's permission. Tenant agrees to pay any costs and attorney fees incurred by Landlord in defending any lawsuit or other action brought in regard to such injuries or damage.

All personal property in the premises is at Tenant's risk only and Landlord shall not be liable for any damages to it, nor is Landlord responsible for insuring Tenant's personal property.

15. Destruction of Premises. In the event more than half of the premises is destroyed by fire or other loss, Landlord and Tenant agree that this Lease shall become void at the option of either Landlord or Tenant.

16. Default. If Tenant makes any default on this Lease, it shall be lawful for Landlord and his representatives and agents to re-enter and repossess the premises, or evict Tenant in the manner prescribed by law. Waiver of any default by the Landlord shall not be construed as a waiver of any subsequent default.

17. Access. Tenant shall allow Landlord access to the premises for purposes of repair and inspection. Landlord shall exercise this right of access in a reasonable manner. Landlord shall give Tenant reasonable notice before exercising this right of access, except in case of emergency.

18. Notice. All notices required by this Lease shall be provided in writing, mailed to the parties as follows:

IF TO LANDLORD: 4593 Clear View Road
Lakewood, OH 44156

IF TO TENANT: 190 Oak St., Apt 4B
Cleveland, OH 44111

19. Parties Bound. This Lease and the promises and agreements it contains shall be binding on the respective heirs, successors, representatives, agents and assigns of the parties.

20. Complete Agreement. This Lease is the complete and final agreement of Landlord and Tenant in regard to the premises described in the Lease. This Lease supersedes any oral or written agreements regarding these premises.

WARNING: THIS LEASE IS A BINDING LEGAL AGREEMENT. YOU SHOULD NOT SIGN IT UNLESS YOU UNDERSTAND IT COMPLETELY. CONSULT WITH AN ATTORNEY FOR ASSISTANCE.

Dated this _____ day of _____, 19____.

LANDLORD:

WITNESS _____   _____

_____

TENANTS:

WITNESS _____   _____

_____

_____

_____

Defective Product Complaint Letter

Document Summary

The Defective Product Complaint Letter allows you to notify a retailer or manufacturer of a defect in an item you have purchased. Although you can use it as a first notice of the problem you've encountered, there are other steps you might want to take before using this letter. Your first step might be to simply return the item to the place where it was purchased. Many retailers will exchange the item with little or no discussion. If that proves impossible, this letter allows you to specify the nature of the defect and the solution you expect. In the event that you are still unable to obtain satisfaction, several steps may be available to you, including a complaint to the Better Business Bureau, a small claims court action, or a lawsuit.

You should consult with an attorney about the options available under your state's laws. Your state or local bar association can provide you with a referral to an attorney who can help you.

Questions and Comments

Note: The following describes <u>every</u> question for the Defective Product Complaint Letter. However, during the Question and Answer session, the program will display only those questions relevant to your personal situation.

Consumer   **Enter your name as you intend to sign this letter.**

[Example: Mary B. Smith]

Comment: Do not use any nicknames or abbreviations.

Consumer Addr   **Enter your street address.**

[Example: 1270 Anystreet, Suite 135]

Comment: If the street address is more than one line, use commas to separate each part.

Consumer CSZ   **Enter your city, state and zip code.**

[Example: Jacksonville, MS 98139]

Comment: Use the name of the community as named by the United States Post Office. Do not use the name of a real estate subdivision unless it is used as a Post Office address.

Enter the city, state, zip code. Use the two-letter state abbreviation, and use at least the five digit zip code. The state abbreviations are listed under *Help Topics*.

Letter Date   **Enter the date you intend to send this letter.**

[Example: 09/28/91]

Comment: Use the MM/DD/YY format. It is not necessary to spell out the date.

Store   **To which store or manufacturer are you sending this letter?**

[Example: Nancy's Discount]

Comment: Both the store and the manufacturer are responsible for product defects. For convenience, it may be easier to deal with the local store from which you purchased the defective product.

Your efforts to get satisfaction when you have purchased a defective product may begin with a return trip to the store or a telephone call to the manufacturer's toll free number. If these efforts produce no result, you may choose to put your dissatisfaction into writing. This letter is intended to serve as the first written notice of your complaint sent to the store from which you purchased the product or to the manufacturer. It is important to keep the original receipt and include a copy of the receipt with the letter. Be sure to keep copies of the letter for your reference.

Store Addr   **Enter the street address of the store.**

[Example: 1270 Anystreet, Suite 135]

Comment: If the street address is more than one line, use commas to separate each part.

Store CSZ **Enter the city, state and zip code of the store.**

[Example: Seattle, WA 98139]

Comment: Use the name of the community as named by the United States Post Office. Do not use the name of a real estate subdivision unless it is used as a Post Office address.

Purchase Date **On what date was the defective product purchased?**

[Example: 09/28/91]

Comment: Use the MM/DD/YY format. It is not necessary to spell out the date.

Purchaser **Identify the person who made the actual purchase.**

[Example: I
my daughter]

Comment: If you purchased the defective product, enter "I". If the purchaser was someone in your family, enter that person's relationship to you (e.g., "my husband", "my daughter", etc.).

Product **Describe the product.**

[Example: a white, travel size Lotsa Curls curling iron (Model C8)]

Comment: Describe the article completely. Include the model, size, color and any other distinguishing characteristics.

If the letter is not being directed to the manufacturer, include the manufacturer's name as well.

Store Loc **Enter the name and location of the store from which the product was purchased.**

[Example: Nancy's Discount at Southend Mall]

Comment: Provide the name of the store and the store's location.

If the letter is being directed to a local store or manufacturer, the location may take the form of a mall or intersection (for example: "Willie's Market at Main Street Mall"). If the letter is not being sent to a local company, the location should include the city and state (for example: "Willie's Market at Main Street Mall in Cleveland, Ohio").

Payment Method **Identify how the product was paid for.**

( ) Check
( ) Cash
( ) Credit card

Comment: When a credit card has been used, it may take some weeks before a credit appears on your bill. Make your selection. Select <NEXT> or press [Enter] to move to the next question.

Defect **In one or two complete sentences, describe the product defect.**

[Example: The curling iron my daughter purchased failed to heat up. Despite testing it at several electrical outlets, the heat sensor light failed to turn colors from red to black.]

Comment: Be specific in your description. Simply saying, "It didn't work," fails to provide adequate information regarding the nature of the defect.

Action Defect **In one or two complete sentences, identify what action you expect the store or manufacturer to take.**

[Example: Please send me a replacement curling iron, and arrange for the return of the defective one. If this is not possible, I expect a full refund of the purchase price.]

Comment: The seller or manufacturer has the right to replace or repair the defective product. You have a right to a refund only if the repair or replacement cannot be reasonably made.

Phone Day **Enter a telephone number at which you can be reached during the day.**

[Example: 242-555-1270]

Comment: Be sure to include the area code. The store or manufacturer may have questions regarding your complaint.

If you fail to receive a response to your letter, you may choose to follow up in writing. Any follow-up letter should reference all steps taken to date to resolve the problem. Send any follow-up letter by certified mail, return receipt requested. If you fail to receive a response to your correspondence, you may want to discuss your options with an attorney.

Letterhead   **Will you be printing this letter on letterhead?**

( ) YES
( ) NO

Comment: Selecting "NO" will cause the program to print your return address at the top of the document. Selecting "YES" will add blank lines to accommodate letterhead paper.

Sample Document[1]

1245 Oak Tree Lane
Jacksonville, MS 71234

October 1, 1991

Nancy's Discount Mart
4593 Main St.
Jacksonville, MS 71245

RE: Defective Product

Dear Sir or Madam:

On August 27th, 1991, my daughter purchased a white, travel size Lotsa Curls curling iron (Model C38) at Nancy's Discount Mart at Southland Mall. The product was paid for by check. I have enclosed a copy of the receipt.

The curling iron my daughter purchased failed to heat up. Despite testing it at several electrical outlets, the heat sensor light failed to turn colors from red to black.

Please send me a replacement curling iron, and arrange for the return of the defective one. If this is not possible, I expect a full refund of the purchase price.

You may contact me at the above address or, during the day, at (409) 555-1234.

I am certain that this matter can be satisfactorily resolved and look forward to your prompt response.

Sincerely,

Martha B. Smith

---

[1] The sample document has been prepared and formatted for illustration purposes only. The actual document will print using the standard type style of your printer and the number of lines per page may differ.

Glossary of Terms

account	A written statement of money transactions, such as credits, debits, deposits, withdrawals and the like.
accrue	To increase or accumulate, as with monetary payments.
accrued interest	Interest which has been earned but which has not yet been paid.
affidavit	Sworn written statement witnessed by a notary public.
agreement	A coming together of two or more parties who assent to do something or incur some mutual obligation to one another.
assignee	One who receives an assignment of the rights and duties of another.
assignment	Transfer by one person to another of the rights and duties described in a contract entered into by the first person.
attestation	Authenticating a document by signing it as a witness.
attorney-in-fact	A person authorized to act on behalf of someone else in business dealings or for other purposes. Authority is given through a power of attorney.
beneficiary	One who is named to receive money or other property, as in an insurance policy or will.

bequest	A gift of money or personal property given through a will.
bill of sale	Document indicating that ownership of property has been transferred from a seller to a buyer.
binding	Imposing a continuing obligation or duty, usually by contract.
bond	A type of insurance whereby a company or an individual agrees to provide reimbursement to another party for any loss suffered due to the actions of a third party.
co-signor	One who guarantees payment of a note in the event the maker, or borrower, fails to pay.
codicils	An amendment to a will, made after the original document is signed and witnessed. Codicils must also be signed and witnessed before they are valid.
community property	Property acquired by a husband and/or wife during their marriage, with each holding a half interest. Only eight states use this method for determining the ownership of property.
competency	The legal ability to perform an act, such as make a Will or enter into a contract.
conservator	A person who is empowered by a court to handle the financial affairs of another.
consideration	Something of value offered as an inducement to enter into a contract.
contest	To challenge the validity of a matter or a document, such as a will.
contract	A legally binding agreement between two or more parties.
corporation	A business organization formed by one or more parties, with rights and liabilities separate from those of the parties that formed it.

covenant	Any written agreement between two parties. In modern use, promises made in the conveyance of real estate.
creditor	One to whom money is owed.
custodian	One who manages a Trust created under the Uniform Transfers to Minors Act. (See Trustee.)
damages	Compensation for loss or injuries suffered due to the acts or omissions of another.
D/B/A	An abbreviation for "Doing Business As".
debtor	One who owes money to another.
declarant	One who makes a declaration; the term used to describe the maker of a Living Will.
default	To fail to fulfill a contractual duty or obligation.
delinquent	Late in fulfilling a contractual obligation, such as falling behind on repayment of a loan.
demand note	A written promise of a borrower to repay the lender at any time the lender requires.
descent and distribution	The method of transferring the property of one who dies without leaving a Last Will and Testament.
disinherit	To deliberately exclude a person from taking anything under a will.
durable power-of-attorney	Authority of one person (the attorney-in-fact) to act on behalf of another (the principal) even if the principal is incompetent and unable to handle his or her own affairs.
duress	Undue force used to pressure a person to take some action he or she would not take otherwise.
encumbrance	Anything which lessens property value or hinders its sale, such as a lien or mortgage.

equal monthly installments	The amount of a loan's principal and total interest, repaid on a monthly basis and calculated by dividing principal and interest by the number of months between the date the loan is made and the date final payment is due.
equal shares	Division of an estate into parts of identical size.
estate	Everything a person owns when he or she dies.
execute	To perform all the acts required. To sign, publish and witness a Last Will and Testament in accordance with the requirements of state law.
executor	Person designated in a will to carry out its terms upon the death of the person making the will.
fee simple	Full and unrestricted ownership of real estate.
gift	Property transferred by one person to another gratuitously and without consideration.
guardian	Someone given legal custody of a person who has been found unable to care for himself or herself.
heir	Any person who takes part of an estate through a person's will.
interest	A charge for borrowing money, generally computed as a percentage of the amount borrowed.
intestate	Without a valid Last Will and Testament.
joint tenancy	A form of property ownership by two or more parties that allows a deceased owner's interest to pass directly to the other owners without the need for probate.
jurisdiction	A court's power to hear and rule on a matter before it.
landlord	The owner of property that is leased or rented to another.

liable	Legally obligated to perform some duty or take responsibility for failing to perform.
lien	A legal claim against property to insure repayment of a debt incurred by the property owner.
living will	Document which directs physicians regarding the withholding or withdrawing of life-prolonging medical procedures in the event of a terminal illness.
maker	One who borrows money on a promissory note.
minor	A person under the legal age of majority, usually under 18 or 21 years old, depending on state law.
notary public	An officer of the state who administers oaths and witnesses signatures on documents.
note	A written promise to pay money to another.
occupant	One who has actual use or possession of a property.
partnership	Agreement of two or more people to operate a business, sharing the profits and the losses.
payee	One to whom money is to be paid, as under a note.
performance	The act of complying with the required terms of a contract.
personal property	Anything a person owns other than real estate.
personal representative	Another term for executor. (See executor.)
per stirpes	"By the roots"; inheritance which goes to the children of a deceased heir as his or her representative.
power of attorney	Document giving one person (the attorney-in-fact) authority to act on behalf of another (the principal).

premises	The subject of a real estate conveyance or lease, such as a building, house or apartment.
pre-payment penalty	Money charged to a borrower to compensate a lender for loss of anticipated interest when a loan is paid before it is due.
principal	1) One who gives authority to another to act on his or her behalf. 2) The amount of money loaned to another.
probate	The judicial determination that the will of a deceased person is valid and genuine.
promissory note	A written promise to pay a specified sum of money to another at some date in the future.
proxy	One who stands in the place of another.
real property	Land and the things permanently fixed to the land, such as buildings and fences.
residuary estate	That part of an estate which remains after all the other provisions of a will have been met.
revocation	An act annulling an earlier act and making it void and unenforceable.
security agreement	Contract giving a lender an interest in some or all of the property of a borrower.
sole proprietorship	Business owned by one person who receives all its profits and is responsible for all its losses.
statute	A law enacted by the legislative branch of government.
successor	One who takes the place of another, assuming the rights and obligations of the first.
tenancy by and with the entirety	Joint ownership of property by husband and wife which allows a deceased spouse's interest to pass directly to the surviving spouse without the need for probate.
tenancy in common	A form of joint ownership of property that allows a deceased owner to pass his or her share in the property by Will.

tenant   One who rents or leases from a landlord and is obligated to make rental payments.

testator   One who makes a will.

trust   A legal arrangement by which one person (the trustee) holds and manages property for the benefit of another.

trustee   The person or institution appointed to manage a trust.

usury   Interest charged to a borrower in excess of a legally established maximum rate.

VIN   Vehicle Identification Number. Used to identify an automobile, truck or other motor vehicle.

void   Without effect.

warrant   A guarantee of title to property and a promise to defend claims made against the property by others.

witness   One who testifies under oath about the acts of another; the act of giving sworn testimony.

Program Error Messages

"Input is out of range."

Check your answer to be sure you filled in a number within the specified range.

"Insufficient disk space."

Problem writing to disk. Check available storage space on your floppy disk or hard disk.

"Insufficient memory."

Home Lawyer requires a personal computer with at least 512K of memory (RAM). Your current system configuration does not leave enough memory for the application to run properly. Remove any background programs before running Home Lawyer again.

"Invalid filename entered; please try again using an 8-character name."

The filename cannot exceed eight characters and cannot contain spaces.

"Invalid state entered."

An invalid two-letter state code was entered. If you are unsure of the code for the state, press [F1], select *Help Topics* and choose *State Abbreviations*.

"Problem with printer. Please check printer and try again."

Check paper supply and printer to insure printer is turned on and is on-line.

"Profile data is not complete. Try again?"

The following fields in the User Profile screen <u>must</u> be completed before saving:
> First Name
> Last Name
> Address 1
> City
> State
> Zip Code

"SYSETUP.DAT could not be found."

The program is unable to locate the requested file. Check available storage space on your floppy disk or hard disk.

"The number of items entered here does not match the prior answer."

The number of items entered here must match the number specified in a previous question. Press [Alt-E] *Edit* and select *Review Answers* to check your previous answers. Add or delete an item accordingly before moving to the next question.

"This question requires an answer."

This question requires that an answer be entered before moving to the next question. If you do not know the answer, enter a question mark (?). You can use the *Edit Answers* option to fill in the correct answer later. (See *Edit Answers* in Chapter 3.)

"Too many windows are open, please close one and try again."

Press [Esc] to close each open window and try again.

Guide to Home Lawyer Support Services

Two types of customer support are available, Monday-Friday, 9:00 a.m. - 5:00 p.m. Eastern time. Here's a description of each for your reference:

Customer Sales & Service

If you have a question about registering your program, purchasing an update to Home Lawyer or any other MECA program, or if you need any other form of non-technical support, these are the folks to call. If you're calling to purchase software or an update, please also tell us the type of computer you're using, and your disk format and be prepared with credit card information. Call us at 1-800-228-MECA or fax us at (203) 256-5159.

Technical Support

If your problem is more technical in nature, our trained staff is prepared to assist you. But before you call, we'd like to ask that you do a few things first.

Read the Help screens. More often than not, it will tell you exactly what you need to resolve a problem.

Check the Reference Manual. It's an excellent reference for commonly asked questions.

If you're still confused, try a little good old-fashioned trial and error. If you make a mistake, you can always leave the program without saving your changes. If you succeed, all the better.

And if all else fails, call Technical Support at (216) 292-3410.

Calling Customer Support

When you do call, please remember to be ready with a brief description of your problem, and:

- The type of your computer

- How much memory you have

- Your DOS version

- Be in front of your computer

- Call us at (216) 292-3410

Registering Home Lawyer

Sending in registration cards on toasters is silly. With software, it's silly not to. Here are just a few of the important reasons why:

- As a registered owner of Home Lawyer, you'll immediately qualify for free Technical Support.

- Your 90 day damaged disk replacement "insurance" will be activated ... just in case your dog acquires a taste for plastic.

- We'll keep you informed about important improvements and enhancements to the program.

State Bar Directory

If you have questions regarding any of the material in this package, you may want to consult with an attorney. If you need assistance in obtaining the name of an attorney in your area, the following list of State Bar Associations is provided for your reference.[1]

Contact your state association at the address and phone number provided and request the attorney referral service. You will be asked the town or city in which you live in and the type of legal matter for which you are seeking assistance. They should be able to provide you with a list of attorneys in your area.

Alabama
Alabama State Bar Association
P.O. Box 671
Montgomery, AL 36101
205-269-1515

Alaska
Alaska State Bar Association
P.O. Box 100279
Anchorage, AK 99510
907-272-7469

Arizona
State Bar of Arizona
363 North First Avenue
Phoenix, AZ 85003
602-252-4804

Arkansas
Arkansas State Bar Association
400 West Markham
Little Rock, AR 72201
501-375-4605

California
State Bar of California
555 Franklin Street
San Francisco, CA 94102
415-561-8200

Colorado
Colorado State Bar Association
1900 Grant Street
Suite 950
Denver, CO 80203
303-860-1112

Connecticut
Connecticut State Bar Association
61 Hungerford Street
Hartford, CT 06106
203-525-8106

Delaware
Delaware State Bar Association
708 Market Street Mall
P.O. Box 1709
Wilmington, DE 19899
302-658-5278

District of Columbia
District of Columbia Bar Association
Suite 600
1707 L Street NW
Washington, DC 20036
202-331-3883

---

[1] This list is accurate as of August 31, 1991. This list is provided for your convenience and is not intended to be an endorsement of the Product by these Bar Associations.

Florida
The Florida State Bar Association
650 Apalachee Parkway
Tallahassee, FL 32399-2300
904-561-5600

Georgia
State Bar of Georgia
800 The Hurt Building
50 Hurt Plaza
Atlanta, GA 30303
404-527-8700

Hawaii
Hawaii State Bar Association
P.O. Box 26
Honolulu, HI 96810
808-537-1868

Idaho
Idaho State Bar Association
P.O. Box 895
Boise, ID 83701
208-342-8958

Illinois
Illinois State Bar Association
424 South Second Street
Springfield, IL 62701
217-525-1760

Indiana
Indiana State Bar Association
230 East Ohio
Indianapolis, IN 46204
317-639-5465

Iowa
Iowa State Bar Association
1101 Fleming Bldg.
Des Moines, IA 50309
515-243-3179

Kansas
Kansas State Bar Association
1200 Harrison
Post Office Box 1037
Topeka, KS 66601-1037
913-234-5696

Kentucky
Kentucky State Bar Association
West Main at Kentucky River
Frankfort, KY 40601
502-564-3795

Louisiana
Louisiana State Bar Association
Attorney Referral Not Offered

Maine
Maine State Bar Association
124 State Street
P.O. Box 788
Augusta, ME 04332
207-622-7523

Maryland
Maryland State Bar Association
520 West Sayette Street
Baltimore, MD 21201
301-685-7878

Massachusetts
Massachusetts State Bar Association
20 West Street
Boston, MA 02111
617-542-9103

Michigan
State Bar of Michigan
306 Townsend Street
Lansing, MI 48933
517-372-9030

Minnesota
Minnesota State Bar Association
430 Marquette Avenue
Suite 403
Minneapolis, MN 55401
612-333-1183

Mississippi
Mississippi State Bar Association
643 North State Street
P.O. Box 2168
Jackson, MS 39225
601-948-4471

Missouri
The Missouri Bar Association
P.O. Box 119
Jefferson City, MO 65102
314-635-4128

Montana
State Bar of Montana
P.O. Box 577
Helena, MT 59624
406-442-7660

Nebraska
Nebraska State Bar Association
635 South 14th Street
Lincoln, NE 68508
402-475-7091

Nevada
Nevada State Bar Association
201 Las Vegas Blvd., South
Las Vegas, NV 84101
702-382-2200

New Hampshire
New Hampshire State Bar Association
112 Pleasant Street
Concord, NH 03301
603-224-6942

New Jersey
New Jersey State Bar Association
1 Constitution Square
New Brunswick, NJ 08901-1500
201-249-5000

New Mexico
State Bar of New Mexico
P.O. Box 25883
Albuquerque, NM 87125
505-842-6132

New York
New York State Bar Association
One Elk Street
Albany, NY 12207
518-463-3200

North Carolina
North Carolina State Bar Association
P.O. Box 25908
Raleigh, NC 27611
919-828-4620

North Dakota
State Bar Association of North Dakota
P.O. Box 2136
Bismarck, ND 58502
701-225-1404

Ohio
Ohio State Bar Association
1700 Lakeshore Dr.
Columbus, OH 43216-0562
614-487-2025

Oregon
Oregon State Bar Association
5200 SW Meadows Road
Lake Oswego, OR 97035
503-620-0222

Oklahoma
Oklahoma State Bar Association
P.O. Box 53036
Oklahoma City, OK 73152
405-524-2365

Pennsylvania
Pennsylvania State Bar Association
100 South Street
P.O. Box 186
Harrisburg, PA 17108
717-238-6715

Puerto Rico
Puerto Rico State Bar Association
No Listing Available

Rhode Island
Rhode Island State Bar Association
115 Cedar St.
Providence, RI 02903
401-421-5740

South Carolina
South Carolina State Bar Association
950 Taylor Street
Columbia, SC 29201
803-799-6653

South Dakota
State Bar of South Dakota
222 East Capitol
Pierre, SD 57501
605-224-7554

Tennessee
Tennessee State Bar Association
3622 West End Avenue
Nashville, TN 37205
615-383-7421

Texas
State Bar of Texas
P.O. Box 12487
Capital Station
Austin, TX 78711
512-463-1463

Utah
Utah State Bar Association
645 South 200 East
Salt Lake City, UT 84111
801-531-9077

Vermont
Vermont State Bar Association
Post Office Box 100
Montpelier, VT 05601
802-223-2020

Virginia
Virginia State Bar Association
Suite 1000
801 East Main Street
Richmond, VA 23219-2900
804-786-2061

Washington
Washington State Bar Association
2001 6th Avenue
500 Westin Building
Seattle, WA 98121
206-448-0441

West Virginia
West Virginia State Bar Association
State Capital Complex
Charleston, WV 25305
304-346-8414

Wisconsin
State Bar of Wisconsin
Post Office Box 7158
Madison, WI 53707
608-257-3838

Wyoming
Wyoming State Bar Association
Post Office Box 109
Cheyenne, WY 82003
307-632-9061

Index

A

About 3-27
    the Home Lawyer Advisor 1-5
Adoption 4-7
Advisor Menu 1-5, 3-34
Applying for a Job 4-8
Automobile
    Accidents 4-9
    Buying New 4-9
    Buying or Selling Used 4-9
    Insurance 4-9
    Leasing 4-9
    Lemon Laws 4-9
    Warranties 4-9
    You and Your 4-9

B

Bad Check Notice 8-19
Bankruptcy and Its Alternatives 4-9
Being A Homeowner 4-6
Being A Juror 4-10
Being A Witness 4-10

Bills of Sale 9-1
Business
    Owning Your Own 4-8
Buying
    A New Car 4-9
    Buying and Selling a Home 4-6
    Buying or Selling A Used Car 4-9
    by Mail 4-8

C

Customer Support C-2
Cancel 3-39
Car Warranties 4-68
Caring for a Parent 4-7
Changing
    an Answer 3-12
    Your Will 4-5
Consumers' Rights 4-8

Child
    Custody and Visitation Rights 4-7
    Support 4-7
Civil Court Procedures 4-10
Complaint
    When You Have A 4-8
Consenting to Medical Treatment 4-10
Consumer
    Contracts 4-8
    Credit Protection 4-9
    For More Information 4-8

Contents of This Package 2-1
Contesting a Will 4-5
Credit
    and Collections 8-1
    Establishing 4-9
Customer Sales & Service C-1
Customer Support 3-23
Customer Support Plan C-1

D

Defective and Unsafe Merchandise 4-8
Defective Product Complaint Letter 11-1
    Document Summary 11-1
    Questions and Comments 11-1
    Sample Document 11-6
Demand for Money Owed 8-13
    Document Summary 8-13
    Questions and Comments 8-13
    Sample Document 8-18

Discrimination 4-6
Dividing Your Property 4-7

Divorce
    and Custody 4-7
    Process 4-7
Document Descriptions 3-8
Document Table of Contents 1-2, 3-6
Documents Menu 3-6
Door-to-Door Sales 4-8
DOS Shell 3-27
Drinking And Driving 4-9
Dying Without a Will 4-5

E

Edit
  Answers 3-29
  Menu 3-28
Editing Key Summary 3-10
Employee Benefits 4-8
Employment Agreement 7-1
  Document Summary 7-1
  Questions and Comments 7-2
  Sample Document 7-6
Employment Forms 7-1
Entering
  an Answer 3-8
  Dates 3-11
  States 3-11
Error Messages B-1
Establishing
  Credit 4-58
  Trusts 4-11
Estate Planning Worksheet 5-1
Evictions 4-27
Exit 3-27
Expand 3-36
Explain 3-37

F

File Menu 3-16
Finding the Right Lawyer 4-11
Funerals and Burials 4-5

G

General Bill of Sale 9-8
  Document Summary 9-8
  Questions and Comments 9-9
  Sample Document 9-12
General Power of Attorney 6-1
  Document Summary 6-1
  Questions and Comments 6-3
  Sample Document 6-8
Getting Started 2-1
Glossary of Terms 3-39, A-1
Going to Court 4-10
  Conclusion 4-10
Guardian
  Naming 4-5
Guide to Home Lawyer Support Services C-1

H

Heirs
  Naming Your 4-5
Home
  Owning Your Own 4-6
Home Lawyer
  Advisor 4-1
  Documents 1-2
  What is? 1-1
How To Avoid Probate 4-5
Hyatt Legal Services 1-1

I

Independent Contractor Agreement 7-9
Installing Home Lawyer 2-1

J

Job Discrimination 4-54
Judicial System, Our 4-10

L

Landlords
  and Tenants 4-6
  Rights 4-6
Last Will and Testament 5-8
  Document Summary 5-8
  Questions and Comments 5-11
  Sample Document 5-27
  Special Considerations 5-9
Lawyers' Ethics 4-11
Leasing
  a Car 4-9
  Residential Property 4-6
Legal Fees and Expenses 4-11
Lemon Laws 4-9
Living Will 5-34, 4-5
  Document Summary 5-34
  Questions and Comments 5-36
  Sample Document 5-40

M

Making a Will 4-5
Marriage 4-7
MECA Software 3-23

Medical
  Malpractice 4-10
  Medical Rights 4-10
Medical/Special Power of Attorney 6-12
  Document Summary 6-12
  Questions and Comments 6-14
  Sample Document 6-19
Motor Vehicle Bill of Sale 9-1
  Document Summary 9-1
  Questions and Comments 9-2
  Sample Document 9-6
Moving Around with
  a Mouse 3-3
  the Keyboard 3-4

N

Naming
  a Guardian 4-5
  Your Heirs 4-5

O

Offer of Employment Letter 7-17
Our Judicial System 4-10
Owning Your Own
  Business 4-8
  Home 4-6

P

Payment Problems 4-9
Personal Law Interview 3-35, 4-1
  Document Summary 4-1
  Questions and Comments 4-1
Personal Law Topics 3-35, 4-5
  Consumers' Rights 4-8
  Divorce and Custody 4-7
  Going to Court 4-10
  Landlords and Tenants 4-6
  Medical Rights 4-10
  Owning Your Own Home 4-6
  When You Need A Lawyer 4-11
  Wills and Trusts 4-5
  You and Your Automobile 4-9
  You, Your Family, and the Law 4-7
  Your Credit 4-9
  Your Job or Business 4-8

Personal Loans 4-9
Powers of Attorney 6-1
Prenuptial Agreements 4-7
Print 3-38
  Document 3-16
  Document to Screen 3-18
  Worksheets 3-30
  to a File 3-19
  to a Printer 3-18
Product Information 3-22
Program Error Messages B-1
Promissory Note 8-1

Q

Question and Answer Session 3-8

R

Register Your Program 3-23
Registering Home Lawyer C-2
Request for Credit Report 8-24
  Document Summary 8-24
  Questions and Comments 8-24
  Sample Document 8-30
Request for Credit Report Correction 8-31
  Document Summary 8-31
  Questions and Comments 8-31
  Sample Document 8-34
Residential Lease 10-1
  Document Summary 10-1
  Questions and Comments 10-2
  Sample Document 10-10
Review Answers 3-29
Revocation of Living Will 5-42
  Document Summary 5-42
  Questions and Comments 5-42
  Sample Document 5-45
Revocation of Power of Attorney 6-22
  Document Summary 6-22
  Questions and Comments 6-23
  Sample Document 6-25
Rights
  As a Patient 4-10
  to Die 4-10
  to Life 4-10

S

Saving Your Answers 3-12
Security Deposits 4-6
Selecting
    a Credit Card 4-9
    a Document 3-7
    a Response 3-11
Settling Your Estate 4-5
Setup 3-24
Shell to WP 3-33
Small Claims Court 4-10
Spousal Support 4-7
State Bar Associations 3-40
State Bar Directory D-1
Steps to Using Home Lawyer 3-5
Structure of This Manual 2-2
System Setup 3-26

T

Technical Support C-1
Telephone Sales and Scams 4-8
Tenants' Rights 4-6
Types of Divorce 4-7
Trusts
    Establishing 4-5

U

Unmarried Couples 4-7
Unwed Parents 4-7
User Profile 3-24
Using
    Help 3-1
    Home Lawyer 3-1
    Your Saved Answers 3-14

W

When You Need A Lawyer 4-11
What is Home Lawyer? 1-1
When You Have A Complaint 4-8
Why You Should Have a Will 4-5
Wills and Trusts 4-5
    Contesting a Will 4-5
    Why You Should Have a Will 4-5
Wills and Living Wills 5-1
Workers' Compensation 4-8

Y

You and Your
    Automobile 4-9
    Family, and the Law 4-7
    Credit 4-9
    Estate 4-5
    Executor 4-5
    Job or Business 4-8
Your Rights As a Patient 4-10